Notes from a Mozambique Prison

Hugh Friberg

Waller Publishing

Nampa, Idaho

Cover Photograph by: Robbie Cracker

Drawings by: Hugh Friberg

Photos: Don Milam

Printed in the United States of America

Table of Contents

Foreword

I am honored to write this foreword for Dr. Hugh Friberg's book, *Notes from a Mozambique Prison*. I have known Dr. Friberg for many years and have always been impressed by his intelligence, creativity, and passion for missions and theology.

My family instilled in me a deep appreciation for missionaries, and I often listened to my grandmothers tell stories of the sacrifices they made to spread the gospel.

I first met Dr. Friberg when I was just a child. He became someone from whom I got to learn firsthand about the difficulties that often befall missionaries. It was no longer stories from the past, but I was somehow experiencing this reality in my own time.

Dr. Friberg's book is a powerful and moving account of his journey with the Lord, which led him to the mission field in Mozambique. You will also learn how he and his family were called to remain and serve during a season of persecution of the church. The book includes an account of his imprisonment because of the gospel. It was a difficult season for the Fribergs, yet at the same time a story of faith, hope, and perseverance in the face of persecution. He never gave up hope, even when confronted with great adversity. Hugh's story is a reminder that even in the darkest of times, there is always light.

This is also an account of a family who dedicated their lives to doing God's will with a desire to see lives transformed by the power of the gospel. That Hugh and Evelyn returned to Africa after his imprisonment to serve in Eswatini made me appreciate them even more as people of great faith and compassion.

This book is a treasure for the followers of Christ. We all encounter difficulties every so often, which sometimes may lead us to frustration, and even to wondering if there is any hope for the future. Here is strong evidence that God is faithful even in those challenging seasons when we don't seem to have clear answers to our questions and frustrations. The accounts in this book will encourage and propel us forward to be faithful stewards of faith that often is received at a high cost.

For those of us from Mozambique, this book provides us with a part of our history that we had not heard. Many of us have wondered if it would be possible to someday hear or learn a few details of the experiences and the challenges faced by the missionaries who were imprisoned during the Mozambique revolution years.

I am grateful for Hugh's courage to share his story. It is a story that needs to be told, and I believe it will encourage and inspire others, who are facing persecution for their faith, to hold on to hope and be reminded that God is fulfilling his plan to restore His creation. There is nothing that will stop the Lord's redemptive work. Despite the persecution, the church in Mozambique didn't stop. God tremendously blessed the ministry that missionaries helped establish and develop. The church there recently celebrated its 100th anniversary—another powerful witness to God's faithfulness.

I highly recommend this book to you. It is a must-read for anyone interested in learning more about God's faithfulness in times of adversity.

Dr. Fili Chambo
General Superintendent
Church of the Nazarene

Preface

Decades ago, I started to tell this story. People would ask if it had been written down. It hadn't. Not yet. "Life" and other responsibilities kept getting in the way, so the diary and notes sat in their box, following us around.

One day after we'd been in the States a few months, black and white photos appeared in the mail from Don Milam. A camera had appeared in the prison early in our imprisonment, though none of us seems to remember the details of how it got there. He had found the roll of film in his things, had them developed, and had shared the photos of us. These images below are among the only physical evidence of our experience. Since that time the film and original images have disappeared. Some of the drawings found below are some that I drew while in prison. Finally, a few years ago, after starting to tell the story again, I began to work on putting it to paper. Two dear friends, Gary Waller (retired NNU professor) and Randy Craker (retired pastor and district superintendent) not only urged me to finish the project, but they also helped make it happen by reading and critiquing. Colleague Amy Crofford helped me answer the big question: "To whom is the story told?" And Jeanne helped untangle my thoughts by careful attention to my words.

So, thanks to those who requested the book and those who helped bring it to the printers. But mostly, my thanks to my wife Evelyn, who has been so patient, and Gayla, Mike, and Lynnee, and six wonderful grandkids—Jonathan, Timothy, Ruby Mae, Samuel, Grahm, and Lydia, for whom the story will help explain "Pop-Pop." Thanks as well to brothers and sisters on both sides of the family. You have waited a long time for the project to be completed.

Sixth Sunday of Easter 2023, Nampa, Idaho

1
Beginnings

I remember it was a Sunday evening, and I had never felt so alone. Looking back across the courtyard of the prison and above the grim, confining wall, I strained to see the second-floor apartment that I had so recently shared with my wife and young family. Fear can't begin to describe what I was experiencing. My world had suddenly been turned upside down and now I found myself inside a prison. Me! A Nazarene missionary! How could this happen? I felt like I was on the far side of a giant chasm and my wife and two children, and my church family were on the opposite side.

Two other missionaries from the United States had been arrested in Maputo, Mozambique. I knew that evening my church family would be gathering to pray fervently for the three of us and our families. That helped, but the loneliness was almost overpowering.

This was the beginning of long months of wondering and waiting. One of the ways I passed the hours, especially on Sunday evenings during incarceration, was revisiting the events of my lifetime that had brought me to this time and place.

The story starts with the spiritual heritage of my mother's family, the Cyrus Bittlestons. Granddad Cyrus and his family moved to northern Idaho early in the 20th century where he farmed a small holding during the summer and logged during the winter.

Revival swept across northern Idaho, and, as a result, they became Christians and faithful members of the Coeur d'Alene congregation of the Pilgrim Holiness Church. Granddad would finish his chores early on Sundays and during revival meetings, hitch up the horses, and drive the family in the wagon the seven miles to town for services. With a family of eight children, he and Grandmother took seriously their task of raising them as believers. My mother Hazel was the fifth child in the family.

My dad, Raymond Friberg, with his parents and siblings, moved from northeast Montana and rented the farm next to the Bittlestons. The Bittleston family welcomed him into their lives.

He was a little rough cut. The Bittlestons told of Dad's coming to school with them on the first day with a freshly washed face, but with dirt on his neck and behind his ears. Apparently, his mother had instructed him to be sure to wash his face before heading to school.

Though Dad had grown up in a home with little spiritual focus, he was drawn in by these godly neighbors. He and his younger brother were both saved under this influence, and it was in this context that Dad felt the call to ministry.

As a high schooler, Dad heard a missionary serving in Argentina speak. He wondered if the Lord was calling him to go to South America. He never served outside North America, but he never forgot being drawn to missionary service. He and Mother, with the Lord's help, surrounded us children from an early age with a focus on missions.

A few years later, after several members of the Bittleston family became Nazarenes, Jerry Johnson came to pastor the Coeur d'Alene Nazarene congregation. In later years, Dr. Johnson held a leadership role in which he became influential in our Mozambique experiences.

The move to the Nazarenes not only provided a church home but also a heritage of education. The Church of the Nazarene has had a deep interest in educating her youth and established a college in Nampa, Idaho, Northwest Nazarene College (NNC). My mother and several of her seven sisters and brothers attended NNC, and, once again, my dad followed the Bittleston kids.

In 1942, during their college years, Mother and Dad were married, and I was born in 1943. After graduation from NNC in 1945, Dad took a pastorate in rural Southeast Wyoming. Once, when I was a toddler, I wandered out of the house into a wheat field around the parsonage and became lost. The whole community turned out to look for this little tow-headed boy. The story was repeated down through the years that God had spared my life for His work.

During my early years, I also came down with pneumonia followed by eczema, gingivitis ("trench mouth"), and diphtheria. I eventually recovered from all of these, though it ultimately required a move to Chinook, Montana, where I could obtain further medical treatment. God provided a pastoral assignment for Dad there, near where family members lived and farmed. Friendships were formed that remain to this day. God's continuing care was evident.

It was in Dad's next assignment in Fairview, Montana, on the Montana-North Dakota border, that I began school. My first-grade teacher was a believer and a member of the nearby Williston, North Dakota, Church of the Nazarene. There was no kindergarten program in town, so I was placed in a first-second grade combined class. Miss Forthun early instilled in me a love of learning, especially reading. This gave me a strong foundation which has served me well in life.

Mother and Dad saw that biographies of exemplary Christians were easily accessible, and I was introduced to stories of missionaries. One I remember well was *Hudson Taylor's Spiritual Secret* about his pioneering work, founding the China Inland Mission. The stories of hardship and sacrifice made a deep impression on me.

Any time missionaries were anywhere within driving distance, Mother and Dad would see to it that I was present to hear and to meet them. I never felt pressured to choose cross-cultural missions as my ministry, but I was surrounded by great men and women of faith whose lives God used to point me in that direction.

A spiritually impactful event during my childhood was the sickness and subsequent healing of our only sister, Jan, when she was three. We were living in Riverton, Wyoming, where Dad was pastoring. She awakened one morning unable to walk. She was rushed to the nearest hospital which was in Casper, and doctors determined that she had contracted rheumatic fever. She was sick for a long time, but her recovery accelerated when our district superintendent and a visiting evangelist prayed for her healing. This time of prayer, added to our congregation's and family's frequent prayer, was a turning point for her.

The doctor expressed concern that she'd not be able to move about normally or have children, but God's healing touch gave her an active life. She and her husband raised a happy, healthy family of five. Our family has always attributed the miracle of her healing to the prayers of God's people and His touch on her life. Little did I know that this foundation of prayer would sustain me during my own difficult days.

****

As already noted, one of the greatest influences in my life was the presence of missionaries in our home and church. When I was nine years of age, Louise Robinson (later Mrs. J. B. Chapman), former missionary and secretary of the denomination's mission organization, was a guest in our home and spoke at the local church my dad pastored. She told of growing up in Washington State, being called to missionary service, and serving in the Kingdom of Swaziland; however, her stories of snakes and lepers convinced me that I didn't want to serve there! And yet, her stories created not only an early love for cross-cultural evangelism, but also a desire to care for the lives and bodies of those being invited into the Kingdom of God.

As a result, I grew up in a world seeing and reading examples of how evangelism, compassion, and justice ministries can be practiced together. I later learned that in some circles, Christians felt the missionary task was "evangelism first and that only." This hadn't been my experience.

My exposure to different cultures was not only through missionary stories. Growing up in Montana and Wyoming, we Friberg kids were very aware that Native Americans lived nearby. The "Indian" children were in the same classrooms with us. They were being assimilated into a US English-speaking culture. We were always curious about these children, wondering about their history and customs. This was years before television service reached the communities where we lived, and we didn't attend movies, so the popular concepts found in playing "Cowboys and Indians" weren't a part of our lives.

In a similar vein, I can clearly remember the first Asian person I had ever seen, walking down the street in our small Wyoming town.

Though there was limited contact, having these experiences made us very aware that we lived in a world in which not everyone looked and acted as we did. Being in this multicultural environment when young and impressionable added yet another influence toward a life of missions.

We moved to Washington State when I was in middle school. As I was finishing my high school studies in suburban Seattle, Mother and Dad felt the direction of the Lord to plant a new congregation in Bellevue, a city next to Kirkland where they were then ministering. We five Friberg children joined in the project, which turned out to be crucial to our discipleship. We went from being ministered to, to being very active in ministry, which helped us all grow.

It was at this time that another event happened in my life which confirmed God's protection. I was heading for home after a Youth for Christ club event, when suddenly I became aware that the brakes weren't engaging! At the bottom of the hill was a T-junction. There was no way I could slow down for a turn, let alone avoid a collision with any on-coming traffic. I am grateful no one was coming down the road. I crashed into the trees but escaped serious injury.

That same afternoon my sister experienced a blockage of the nerves in her face which caused temporary paralysis. She had to wonder how serious a condition this was and if she would have to deal with it for the rest of her life. These were big questions for a young girl.

We went through those ordeals with few long-term effects, and the whole family experienced a great deal of gratitude to God.

These memories of the influences in my life filled the long, lonely hours in that cramped prison, as I waited for word of release.

2
College and Seminary Years

Brought back out of my musings to the realities of the present, I again became aware of the five hundred men crowded in prison with me from many ethnicities and countries. With inadequate sanitation facilities and cramped cells, daily life was dreary. I so looked forward to the visits of friends and acquaintances who brought food and encouragement. Some, however, would pour out the frustrations and realities of life under Marxist-Leninism. I was especially troubled by the uncertainty of our status and the timing of our questioning by authorities. No visible follow-up and very few releases kept the question alive: "What is happening?" This and many questions were without answers. While I waited, I continued reflecting on my journey.

Northwest Nazarene College

My dad had been my only pastor, but in college I had different voices speaking into my life. It is hard to overemphasize God's impact through our pastor, Earl Lee, and his wife, Hazel. The Lees were former missionaries, having served in India. They shared memorable experiences from their time there, especially a time of transformative revival. Hazel's deeply impactful Sunday school class and Pastor Lee's practical and memorable pulpit ministry—as well as personal friendship with students attending NNC and Nampa First Church of the Nazarene—enabled us to grow as disciples of Jesus. Their daughter, Gail, became a close friend of Evelyn Young, whom I had begun dating. Gail was the head of the fourth grade Sunday school department in which I taught for a year.

After Evelyn and I met, we slowly eased into a relationship that has lasted over fifty years. Our first encounter was when she borrowed a science textbook from me. It didn't take long to learn that she had come from very good people. Her parents were faithful and loyal members of the Medford First Church of the Nazarene in Southern Oregon. Attending church and singing together in the choir was an important part of our dating as we came to know and love each other.

Evelyn didn't feel a special calling to missions but had always been willing to serve. As we contemplated marriage, we wondered if she needed her own sense of calling to cross-cultural missions. One day after chapel at NNC, we were talking with visiting missionaries, Dr. Ken and Ann Stark. They helped us work through this obstacle to our relationship. In the end, Evelyn became a very effective missionary in her own right, having followed the man who had the calling.

Evelyn's background prepared her for our missionary journey together. Both the Nazarene and Missionary Church faith communities encouraged Evelyn's family to get and stay grounded in a holy life with a mission focus. Her grandfather, Ernest Young, was saved and called into ministry in the Missionary Church Association. During his years of ministry, he served as a pastor and a district superintendent in this Wesleyan-Holiness denomination. This put him and his family in close contact with missionaries who had deep fervor for cross-cultural ministry.

One of Evelyn's aunts spent several years in Nigeria as a missionary teacher. Through the years, Aunt Nellie would share stories of God's provision while she was in Africa. One of her favorites was of helping a sick child who longed for a doll. She encouraged the child to pray specifically, and one arrived in a parcel at just the right time!

God was at work during my college years sharpening my leadership skills. I took on roles that helped provide patterns of leadership for life and ministry. Involvement in student government and campus ministries, along with serving as Dr. Joseph Tracy's assistant in the chemistry department, were useful in my training. During high school, I had had little experience in leadership, except for being on the team leading the Youth for Christ club at our school. But college was more geared to my personality. Groups aligned with my interests and skills were available. Ministry trips with Christian Workers' Band, both in Nampa at retirement centers and in various churches served by the college, were formative. Involvement with students and faculty in the science club, taking field trips across the Western United States, as well as class leadership roles, provided opportunities to grow as a leader. I served in Circle K, a student service organization, which provided community-level as well as college-level service opportunities. I benefitted from the time I spent with the great advisors and other students involved in these groups.

Nazarene Theological Seminary

From an early age, it was clear to me that my life's work was missions. For several years, I felt I would be a medical missionary, so I prepared accordingly through high school and college. I even applied to medical school. Visiting Nazarene Theological Seminary (NTS) during my senior year at NNC convinced me that I needed to have at least one year of seminary studies before entering medical missionary service. Even though mathematics and natural science were my major areas of study in college, I didn't find higher level mathematics easy. My interest in people and ministry became increasingly important during these years. When I applied to medical school during my final year of college, my application was not accepted. With the realization that God had a different path for me, I enrolled at NTS and finished the three-year course of study with a focus on world mission.

For many NTS students, the graduate studies were a repetition of what they had done in their college work. But for me, transferring from mathematics and science with only the minimum required subjects in Bible and theology, I found seminary studies exciting and challenging. Much of the work involved research and writing, with exams focused on understanding plus utilization of the subject matter.

Because of my calling to missions, the classes with Dr. Paul Orjala were of particular interest, especially studies in missiology and linguistics. He and his family had served as pioneer missionaries for the Church of the Nazarene in

Haiti, and he brought depth and practical application to his courses. Besides learning from his personal experiences and insights, we were required to read classical as well as current studies in missiology—the Church's response to the Mission of God—and this proved to be especially crucial.

Without dormitories and few student services, the seminary community centered on learning, worship, and creating fellowship. The group of students sensing a calling to cross-cultural ministry, as well as other students and members of our local church, became family to us. The Church of the Nazarene in Shawnee, Kansas, provided rich fellowship and lasting connections that remained fresh through the years. Our understanding of the church grew as we made friends from across the Nazarene and Wesleyan-Holiness world—from North America, Europe, Asia, and Africa. What an exciting mix of people.

Among the professors at NTS, Dr. and Mrs. Delbert Gish (Carol) were significantly important. In exchange for my painting a room in their house, Mrs. Gish offered to make an oil painting from a photo of pre-eruption Mount St. Helens in Washington State, to help us remember the mountains of the Pacific Northwest.

During the time we were in Kansas City, one of Evelyn's sisters, Doris, and her husband, Dan Berg, along with her brother Harold Young and his wife, Linda, moved to the Kansas City area and we three men attended seminary together. Evelyn's brother-in-law served as Dr. Kenneth Grider's teaching assistant. The stories he would pass on added to our enjoyment and sense of appreciation for "Doc" Grider and the rest of our professors. These godly men and women invested in our lives during those formative years, and their consistent ministry gave us patterns for both our pastoral and our missionary work

I was elected secretary of the senior class. Fulfilling the demands of this office while carrying a full class load and working part time made for a very heavy schedule. I fell into a pattern of being constantly busy, and my studies suffered as a result of my tendency to over-commit.

Reflecting on these early days—growing up, attending NNC and NTS, and the various influencers in my life— reminded me of the foundational processes that helped develop in me a dual track of personal maturity and ministry development. Yet they didn't prepare me for life in prison with the intensity of personal issues such as living with fear and uncertainty, as well as the lack of consistency in day-today activities. My, how the Lord uses unusual circumstances to bring us to new levels of maturity.

3
The Journey to the Mission Field

Upon graduation from NTS in 1968, Evelyn and I went to Michigan where I served as associate pastor at the Midland Community Church of the Nazarene. The congregation loved and guided us in ministry, and, after a year, I was asked to fill the lead pastoral role following the resignation of our senior pastor. I served in this capacity for a few months until a new pastor was called. We returned to the Pacific Northwest to take a pastorate in Sumner, Washington, where we spent two years and came to love the congregation. We watched them grow as they made plans to build a larger facility.

While we were in Sumner, we completed the application process for appointment as career missionaries through the Nazarene World Mission Department. In January 1971, we met with the mission leaders and the Board of General Superintendents (BGS). Our interview with the BGS was memorable as Evelyn was asked, "Would you be willing to stick with an overseas mission assignment if or when things got difficult?" Was that prophetic? A few days later, we received a telegram notifying us that we had been appointed to the country of Mozambique in southeast Africa.

During this time, the Mozambique mission director, and, as it turned out, my future cellmate, Armand Doll, was visiting in the Seattle area. We met him and began to get acquainted. We also began to research the history of the country of Mozambique and the work of the Church of the Nazarene there. Though the public library in nearby Tacoma provided clues about the situation in the country, we wished leaders would have filled in more details. We did learn there was a growing struggle for independence from Portugal, but we couldn't begin to grasp the realities of what lay ahead.

Later in the year, we completed our responsibilities with the Sumner congregation and received clear instructions from Rev. Doll and the Mozambique mission council regarding next steps. Our first child, Gayla, was born in July 1971, and we left the United States in December.

The first instruction was to go to Portugal to learn Portuguese because entry into Mozambique depended on it. On our way for language study in Lisbon, we were able to visit Evelyn's sister and her husband, Doris and Dan Berg. They were studying at the University of Glasgow and pastoring the Kilmarnock Church of the Nazarene on the British Isles North District.

Three events stood out in my mind from our short stay: we visited the museum at David Livingstone's birthplace in Blantyre; we had our first East Indian meal; and we met the Kilmarnock Nazarenes.

Livingstone had long been a hero of mine, and we discovered that he had left the British Isles for southern Africa 140 years to the day before our visit to Scotland. All of our years in Africa we enjoyed Indian and Pakistani food whenever we could, and our appreciation of it began in a crowded and steamy restaurant on a cold, rainy night in downtown Glasgow. And while visiting the delightful, warm folks at the Church of the Nazarene in Kilmarnock, we had our first exposure to a form of English other than what we were used to. The children gathered around Evelyn who was holding our five-month-old daughter. One reached up and tugged on her sleeve to let her know that she was being talked to. We felt like we were among friends though we didn't always understand the Scottish brogue.

When we arrived in Lisbon, we were welcomed by Duane and Linda Srader and their two children. The Sraders were studying Portuguese in preparation for their work in the

Cape Verde Islands as Nazarene missionaries. They introduced us to the Nazarene Ambassadors, a Cape Verdian group that met weekly for prayer and fellowship. This group welcomed us to the Portuguese world, and one of the young ladies helped us with our language study. I preached my first sermons in Portuguese —though Pastor João would re-preach my messages to make sure the group understood my halting effort. Quite a humbling learning experience.

We were thrilled to finally land in the capital city of Maputo (formerly Lourenço Marques*) and be greeted by Nazarene missionaries and church leaders. This would be the team we would work with and who would be our friends and support through the challenging days ahead.

*Upon Mozambican Independence in 1975 the city of Lourenço Marques was renamed Maputo. The city will be referenced as Maputo throughout the book.

4

The Church of the Nazarene in Africa

There were times during my incarceration when I would reflect on how the Church of the Nazarene had arrived in Mozambique. Then I would wonder how we three US citizens and our Mozambican colleagues had gotten into this situation.

From their earliest days in Mozambique, Nazarenes had cared for the lost, the least, and the last. This included ministry to lepers on an island in the Limpopo River near the mission station in Tavane. As new missionaries in the country, Glenn and Bessie Grose ministered in this colony on occasional visits. On December 1, 1941, during one those visits, Glenn's boat overturned, and he drowned. Hearing stories like this helped confirm that there was often a cost to following Jesus and ministering in his name. Years later, the Mozambican church honored this sacrifice by naming the church on the Tavane mission station the Glenn Grose Memorial Church of the Nazarene. And the influence continued when Bessie married another young missionary, William C. Esselstyn. He eventually became the regional director, and later, their son, Theodore, was our colleague and "boss" during our years of teaching in Africa.

Nazarene mission work was involved with two main ethnic groups: the African tribe of the Shangaans (or Tsongas) and the ethnic Portuguese. Other smaller people groups such as those speaking Ronga, lived in the area and were also part of the church. Our motivation as a church has always been that everyone needs the opportunity to respond to the Good News, no matter their color, language, or political status. As a result, five Shangaan-speaking districts in southern Mozambique were established by the time we arrived in country.

Not all the work among the Portuguese took place in the metropolitan area around Maputo. Missionaries Floyd and Libby Perkins had enthusiastically followed up leads in other cities in the country, such as Beira and Nampula. We were encouraged to oversee the planting of congregations in these areas. Deep cultural differences and suspicions arising from years of Portuguese cultural, economic, and political domination were at play. The majority of Nazarenes in Mozambique were not conversant in the Portuguese language and shared little of Portuguese culture. Therefore, separate ethnic local churches were planted, and separate districts were formed.

It's easy to look back and criticize the decision to establish separate congregations and districts, but one must truly examine the situation to understand why it happened. Every person of every culture needs to be introduced to the Christ of the gospel, so across Africa people had come to Christ from groups that didn't get along well. This became a problem when these realities were misunderstood by those in leadership who hadn't lived or ministered among these various groups and didn't understand the tribalism that was experienced.

Scattered all over the country were Portuguese-speaking farmers, merchants, and government employees all in need of the gospel message, though most were nominally Christian.

Among the Portuguese-speaking inhabitants of the country were Cape Verdians and others from across the Portuguese Empire who had migrated to Mozambique for economic opportunities. One of the branch Sunday schools in Maputo was held in the home of one of these families. Also, one family from Goa, a Portuguese enclave in India, were a part of the original Portuguese-speaking Church of the Nazarene, and their son, Eduardo, was the associate pastor. Given these various cultures, the ministry of the Church of the Nazarene in Mozambique was diverse and complex.

Those Mozambicans who were conversant with the Portuguese language and assimilated into Portuguese culture, were attracted to the Maputo *Cidade* (City) church which operated in the Portuguese language.

Mozambique

The Republic of Mozambique lies on the southeast coast of Africa, stretching north to south for eighteen hundred kilometers (1000 miles), and across the Mozambique Channel from Madagascar. Prior to the founding of the Portuguese Empire, Mozambique endured several centuries of domination by Arab slave traders.

For most of recorded history, Mozambique was part of the worldwide Portuguese empire. Adventuresome explorers such as Vasco da Gama and Bartolomeu Dias travelled the world and claimed territories for the Portuguese throne stretching from the far west of the Eurasian continent to the Indonesian spice islands. At one time, that empire included the Republic of Brazil until she obtained her independence from Portugal in 1822. The countries of Mozambique, Angola, Cabo Verde, Guinea-Bissau, São Tomé and Príncipe in Africa, Goa and Macau in Asia, and East Timor (*Timor Leste* in Portuguese) in Oceana, obtained their independence from Portugal in the 1970s. For a number of years Mozambique was a province in Portuguese East Africa, but in the early 1970s it was considered a state of Portugal.

The colonial relationship was not always smooth sailing. As socialist countries around the world joined in the East-West struggles of the Cold War, nationalistic groups struggled for freedom and independence from colonial governments. In Mozambique, several organizations vied with each other and against the military-led Portuguese government under successive presidents, António de Oliveiro Salazar and then Marcelo Caetano. The largest of these parties was FRELIMO (the FRont for the LIberation of MOzambique).

In the 1960s and 70s, the Portuguese found themselves—at home and overseas—in a much larger struggle than they had faced before. The resistance to Portuguese rule in Mozambique took on an armed and militant phase, with direct assistance from the neighbor to the north, Tanzania, who provided asylum for dissident Mozambicans. China and Russia promised political and economic assistance. Rising complaints in Portugal against the war of independence—or terrorist war, depending on one's point of view—were on the rise as young men and national resources were being depleted.

The Republic of South Africa used the port of Maputo for shipping goods from her booming economy around Johannesburg. Another neighbor, the break-away government of (Southern) Rhodesia (now called Zimbabwe), under Ian Smith had unilaterally declared independence from Britain a decade earlier. Landlocked Rhodesia depended on the Mozambican port of Beira for her trade. These realities pressured the Portuguese regime in Lisbon toward making decisions about the future of Mozambique. This was the world we entered.

The Church of the Nazarene in Mozambique

The work in Mozambique began early in the history of Nazarene missions in Africa. Rev. and Mrs. Charles Jenkins followed Mozambican miners home in May 1922. The miners had become Christians under the ministry of Nazarene and other evangelists in the Republic of South

Africa. According to Nazarene historian, David Whitelaw, they did so in order to "conserve the fruit" of that evangelism. As the Jenkinses established the work of the church, which was soon centered in Tavane, they were later joined by Glenn and Bessie Grose.

A hundred kilometers (60 miles) north of Xai-Xai, the first Nazarene mission in Mozambique was established by Rev. and Mrs. Jenkins in the community of Njatigwe. At the end of the 1920s, the Portuguese government ruled that all missions had to construct permanent buildings or leave. The Nazarenes had none, but the Methodist mission had decided to relocate and offered their site to the church. Despite the lack of funds because of the world war and the Great Depression, the last-minute decision was made to purchase the site in nearby Tavane before the Church of the Nazarene had to abandon its mission in Mozambique.

The Tavane mission station became the district center for the work in southern Mozambique and was located on the railway line outside the town of Manjacaze in Gaza Province, north of the capital. The local church, Bible college, clinic, and Tavane District Office were located there. Most of the missionaries lived there as well.

Lorraine Schultz directed a Bible training center in Tavane serving the Nazarene, Free Methodist, and Congregational churches in southern Mozambique. The mission station housed a medical clinic staffed by African as well as ex-patriot missionary nurses such as Virginia Benedict, Evelyn Mewes, Heather Howie, and Patricia Buffet who were part of the team who ministered to the mission and surrounding community. A Mozambican pastor, Simeon Mathe, pastored the local church. Armand and Pauline Doll, Frank and Heather Howie, Jakob (Jaap) and Gezina (Ina) Kanis, and Oscar and Marjorie Stockwell, were involved in district development and evangelism.

By the mid-1970s, the church in Mozambique had developed into four national districts in the south of the country, with capable national superintendents: Benjamin Langa, Lot Mulate, João Machava, and Simeão Mandlate, who primarily ministered to Shangaan-Tsonga congregations.

Church planting around Maputo developed as men moved to the city following work opportunities. The number of men in the churches was unique since often African congregations tended to have a large percentage of women and children in attendance. This urban southern district was strong financially and numerically, so it was natural that many men became members and had leading roles. Also, as there were few opportunities for political leadership in the country unless they assimilated to Portuguese language and culture, the church provided an alternate means for service to the community.

When the International Holiness Mission (IHM) of Great Britain joined the Church of the Nazarene in 1952, two mission centers in the north of Mozambique united with the Church of the Nazarene, becoming one district. Former IHM missionary Norman Salmons led this work and, for a few years, Nazarenes Oscar and Margery Stockwell served in Furancungo, near the city of Tete in northern Mozambique. This work among Chichewa-speaking Mozambicans formed another Nazarene district. Rev. Marcelino Rupia was serving as district superintendent at this time.

The work of evangelism and leadership development in South Africa continued among the Mozambican miners. Two missionary couples, Ken and Minnie Singleton and Paul and Mae Hetrick, Sr., and their families, lived and worked in the communities near the mines. The South African mines organization had a very active recruitment program during these years, and the influx of miners provided Christian evangelists many opportunities to lead men to faith in Jesus.

Working alongside the national workers and ex-patriot missionaries in both countries and living in Maputo were Doug and Anne Alexander who developed Shangaan literature, and Fairy Cochlin, who headed up *Mintlawa* ("Groups"), an organization for educating and evangelizing young women.

A sixth district was formed in Mozambique to support evangelism and discipleship among the Portuguese. Many had come to Mozambique to work in government offices or in commercial agriculture. In addition, there were owner-operators of businesses and industries, small and large. Shopkeepers, green grocers, and taxi drivers were all represented in the country. A number of Mozambican Portuguese were able to purchase second homes in the city which they rented out in anticipation of retirement.

The capital city had a central area with government offices and light industrial sites as well as the businesses and shops mentioned above. Most Portuguese residents of the country lived in this area, as well as the nearby suburb of Matola. In these two centers the two larger Portuguese congregations were planted, and buildings built.

When missionaries began to be redeployed in the country, many—including the Alexanders and Miss Cochlin—lived in these residential areas, often in apartment buildings. Near the large apartment complexes were smaller, one- or two-story private residences and shops. The township of Sommershield was the community in which independent missionaries Don and Micki Milam and Assembly of God missionaries Dave and Jan Hall lived, and where Armand and Pauline Doll and our family also lived. The Protestant missionaries met for prayer and fellowship on a regular basis and experienced great cooperation between these ministries.

5
Our Arrival in Mozambique

Imagine our excitement when we were officially appointed to Mozambique in January 1972. It was the fulfillment of all our longings and dreams to be in this context of ministry.

Evelyn and I had spent eighteen months in Portugal learning the language and culture. It was now time to take our young daughter and head to Mozambique for our first missional assignment among the Portuguese-speaking inhabitants of the country. We were one of the last Nazarene missionary couples to arrive in Africa by boat. It turned out that it was cheaper to take the right-hand drive car we had purchased in Europe plus our crate of personal goods, on the passenger ship, than for us to fly and ship the goods separately.

The day we arrived in Mozambique in July 1973 was our daughter Gayla's second birthday. We will never forget it.

We were assigned to take the place of Floyd and Libby Perkins, who had moved to Pretoria, South Africa, where

Floyd was finishing his doctoral studies at the University of South Africa. They had been influential in opening churches among Portuguese-speaking residents of Mozambique and heading up pastoral training among them. Both initiatives were under the jurisdiction of the South African European District, which, along with English-speaking congregations in Central Africa, attempted to advance the holiness message among English and Afrikaans-speaking believers. Our responsibility was to continue the effort with the Portuguese, planting churches and expanding the work among them throughout the country. This ministry had become a separate pioneer district under the Mozambique mission council.

Upon arrival we stayed with Fairy Cochlin in her home on the outskirts of Maputo and then with the Alexander family in the city center. We were waiting for our personal effects and car to be released from customs. We located an apartment, appliances, and furniture, and finally got set up in our own place. All the missionaries gave us a warm welcome.

The car we brought from Europe was a blue Volkswagen station wagon. Upon our arrival, it was impounded. We discovered that the duty was far more than we could pay. So, we went to prayer. The Lord used two important events to get us through this crisis.

First, we heard a sermon by an evangelist speaking at Pasadena First Church of the Nazarene. (This was through Cassettes for Christ, a ministry of Pasadena First Church and our college pastor, Earl Lee.) The evangelist encouraged people with financial needs to give a special tithe. The congregation responded, and so did we to demonstrate our trust in God.

Second, our home district, Washington Pacific, heard of our situation and spread the word. Local congregations took up offerings, and individuals gave to help cover the duty. By the time the bill had to be paid later that month, the car was over a year old, thus reducing the value and amount due. We received all but a few dollars of the total needed. Little did we know how important that little blue vehicle would be in our story. Thanks be to God for His care!

One of its earliest uses was to help with the arrival of our second-born child. In October of 1973, our colleagues and friends strongly encouraged us to go to Pretoria, South Africa, for the birth of our son, Michael, our only Africa-born child. Both girls, Gayla and Lynnée, were born in

Puyallup, Washington, during a pastorate and a home assignment.

Within a year of our arrival, the Revolution of the Carnations took place in Portugal. It was a military coup that overthrew the authoritarian *Estado Novo* regime on April 25, 1974, in Lisbon. A socialist government came to power. The coup led to the Portuguese transition to multi-party democracy and the end of the Portuguese Colonial War. Among the first items on its agenda was to stop the wars in the overseas provinces and territories and grant Independence to these countries. One could almost feel a collective sigh of relief, but with it came a sense of uncertainty since there had been little preparation for it. Discussions soon began, leading to the Lusaka Accord (signed in September 1974), in which Portugal granted independence to Mozambique under the largest of the political parties, FRELIMO, with Samora Machel as party president. Machel became president of both the party and the country upon Independence.

Even though there had not been a referendum leading to the change in government, there was a great deal of excitement and anticipation of a new day. Independence celebrations were scheduled for June 25, 1975, as a

---

provisional government was formed to guide the country toward Independence.

Mission organizations discussed at length whether the ex-patriot missionaries should stay in the country in order to identify with the people or to play it safe by leaving. This major concern was related to the outbreaks that had happened in September and October 1974, when demonstrations and rumors led to riots and violence in the cities, including the capital city. It was following the signing of the Lusaka Accord, and the establishment of the provisional government, that trouble broke out. Thousands of Portuguese and many Mozambicans attempted to derail the Independence process, calling for a free-market economy and a system of government with free elections and multiple parties. This resulted in several deaths and much vandalism as rumors spread. It was said that groups of Mozambicans and Portuguese were killing each other. As a result, many were on edge as Mozambique headed for Independence. It was reported in the media that up to 20,000 Mozambicans and Portuguese fled the country during this time.

In both September and October 1974, the Nazarene World Mission leaders ordered the missionaries to go to South Africa for safety. On one of those occasions, Dr. Jerry

Johnson, the Nazarene World Mission director, was visiting in Mozambique. When rioting broke out in the capital city, three of the missionaries were caught in the fray. The car in which Fairy Cochlin and Ken and Minnie Singleton were riding was surrounded, and the car was stoned. Ken had the presence of mind to put books and boxes beside the heads of the ladies in the front seat. They were able to turn the car around and escape. Though there were injuries and some damage, they survived.

Even so, our letters of the time revealed how frustrating those days were. We wrote that we experienced "defeat and shame" for leaving the country during the difficult days of the riots, "indecision," awareness of "secondary motives," and "stress and anxiety." They were very confusing times, and we were often afraid. However, when the crises passed later in 1974 and many of us returned, both the Portuguese and the African believers welcomed us back. When it came time for the Independence celebrations, we were allowed to make our own decisions.

The Nazarene missionaries were offered options as they related to our futures: we could request reassignment to another field; we could take retirement; or we could stay. Fairy Cochlin returned to the United States to recover from her injuries. The Singletons returned to South Africa to resume their work. It took considerable time to recover from their injuries and the trauma of the attack. Floyd and Libby Perkins moved to Brazil, and Jaap and Ina Kanis transferred to South Africa. We had left twice before during riots and uncertainties and had returned each time when it felt safe. Now we had to make the difficult decision about staying in Mozambique as the time of the Independence celebrations drew near. It was very upsetting to our children to be in this constant state of flux. Evelyn and I felt that our place was to be with the Maputo Portuguese congregation (which I was pastoring) and the Mozambican people during this major transition. So, we stayed in the country. We felt the Lord had promised us safety. My life's Bible passage is Matthew 28:16-20:

> Then the eleven disciples went to Galilee, to the mountain where Jesus had told them to go. When they saw him, they worshipped him; but some doubted. Then Jesus came to them and said, "All authority in heaven and on earth has been given to me. Therefore, go and make disciples of all nations, baptizing them in the name of the Father and of the Son and of the Holy Spirit, and teaching them to obey everything I

have commanded you. And surely, I am with you always, to the very end of the age." (NIV)

This promise that the Lord would be with us felt very personal.

When we had gone to South Africa or Swaziland for safety and people in those countries discovered we were planning to return to Mozambique, many expressed great concern that we were taking unnecessary risks. On one of the returns, there had been enough negative feedback about what could happen, that I experienced a "panic attack" as we travelled toward the border. I wrote to my parents:

The Lord brought to my mind the "Cycle of Victorious Living" (Psalm 37) that we had heard in college from our pastor, Earl Lee. I began to commit our situation, confessing my fear; the Lord really helped me calm down. By the time we reached the border I was able to be quite calm as the soldiers went through "with a fine-tooth comb," just about everything we had, as well as the frustration of having to exchange 65 South African cents (about a dollar) to Mozambican escudos, I was quite calm. After that thorough check, we had no more checks, only an information checkpoint just outside the passport control gate. The other roadblocks between the border and the city had been removed. PTL!

As the socialist and anti-church policies of the new Mozambican government became clearer, more Portuguese fled their homes and jobs to seek new lives in other countries. These were discouraging days, as nearly every week church members and friends left the country. For example, not long after our arrival in Mozambique, Acácio da Cunha Pereira, pastor of the Maputo Portuguese congregation, left for the United States with his wife and daughter. He had received an invitation to work with the Latin Publications Department in the Nazarene World Ministry Center in Kansas City.

Then, Luís Pereira (no family connection to Acácio Pereira), the pastor of the other fully organized Nazarene Portuguese congregation on the Matola district left. He wanted to move into the city over safety concerns and better access to schools. Eventually the uncertainties of the situation in Mozambique led him to Lisbon where he pastored a Nazarene congregation.

The mission council asked us if we would temporarily step into the pastorate of the Maputo congregation that Acácio Pereira had left. So, instead of planting the church in new places, I eventually oversaw several congregations, including the Maputo and the Matola Portuguese congregations and their properties.

Because of a reduction in missionary staff, added responsibilities came my way, including assisting with the literature operation and the theological education by extension program, plus serving on the Mission Council Executive Committee. Along with Armand Doll, I was chosen to represent the Church of the Nazarene on the Christian Council of Mozambique. I continued preaching, teaching, and administering the concerns of the congregation of which I was pastor, all in my second language.

Getting Fairy Cochlin's personal effects sold, and the Perkins' belongings sent to Brazil also fell on my shoulders. The demands of family with a rapidly changing cultural and political environment, along with various bouts of malaria sapped my energy and time.

We felt responsible for the people and the resources entrusted to us. So, even though we were concerned for our personal safety, the Lord's "I will be with you always" provided the stability we needed. Yet, in another letter to my parents, I said, "You cannot imagine the pressure!"

During this confusion, we met a young ethnic Indian who was drawn to the way of Jesus and wanted to be baptized. Joshi had become a believer, and his wife was a seeker. We were able to provide 30 Hindi Bibles for his family and other interested Indians in the city.

When independent US missionary, Don Milam, his family, and some other fine young men moved from Matola into Maputo, they began to attend our Sunday evening worship services. The skills and enthusiasm they brought were a real blessing to the congregation.

Things were becoming more difficult politically. Several weeks before Mozambican Independence (Feb. 19, 1975), I wrote:

> Mozambique is taking some big steps to becoming a socialist/communist country. One of the clearest examples is the universal formation of people's committees who deal with all matters within that area. We even have them in the city, and they will soon have much to say about housing. This week a law was announced that all dwellings left unused for over 3 months will become the property of the government. This probably means that we have lost one of our church buildings, the newest and prettiest, plus the

parsonage and the old parsonage! Our newspapers are full of anti-US propaganda, plus anti-everything that is not communist! It is evident to many of our missionaries that what we are going to do in Mozambique is going to have to be done soon, or it won't be done at all.

In a letter dated June 17, 1975, I wrote to my parents:

The city is really getting decked out nicely for Independence celebrations. It is cleaner than it has been for months! The city is putting up banners in the FRELIMO colors (black, white, red, yellow & green) up and down the main streets, and for the past few weeks they have been planting flagpoles along the major streets as well, in groups of five. I suspect that later this week, or even next week, the new FRELIMO flag will be unfurled, plus the Portuguese flag, perhaps Tanzanian and two others—perhaps Chinese and Russian. All tourists have been banned until the end of the month, except those with special invitations from FRELIMO, including foreign journalists.

A few weeks later (July 6), I added:

> Tuesday night the 24th of June began the real
> Independence celebrations, especially at midnight,
> when several tens of thousands had gathered at the
> big *futebol* stadium in Machava (12 km or so out of
> downtown Maputo) in the rain, to see the lowering of
> the Portuguese flag for the last time and the raising of
> the Mozambique flag for the first. Samora Machel had
> been out of Mozambique for ten years officially,
> though he was army commandant involved in the
> military struggle against the Portuguese. He did a
> rather extensive tour of Mozambique's nine provinces
> made into a film, *"Do Rovuma ao Maputo"* ('From the
> Rovuma to Maputo'). The city gave him a rather
> fantastic reception when he arrived on Monday.
>
> A few minutes after midnight, when the new
> flag was in place and Samora Machel proclaimed
> Mozambique the People's (or Popular) Republic of
> Mozambique, close to our house, and in Machava by
> the stadium, all pandemonium broke loose. We began
> to hear a terrible racket, small rockets, tracer bullets,
> and ammunition (live or blanks, we don't know, but
> the South African news or *Time* reported two people

wounded) being shot into the air from or in front of the prison, and the barracks close by our house. What a display! At first, we had no idea what it was, but feared it was a counter-coup attempt. Off and on until about two in the morning, the celebrations went on, and once again a grand volley went off Independence Day morning when Samora Machel took the oath of office of President. We were listening in on the radio, for we didn't feel it too wise to be in the large jubilant groups in attendance.

On July 3, within a few days after the Independence Day celebrations, Don Milam and his team were arrested, questioned, and put into the city's central prison. The Nazarene congregation was shocked and prayed fervently for their safety and release. Michelle (Micki), Don's wife, was faithful to visit the men and care for their needs. As their pastor, I too was able to visit them. The prison provided simple meals, but families and friends could also bring meals. Coordinating these matters was always a challenge since the only telephone easily available to us was at the church office, a couple of miles away. Armand Doll also had a phone in his office, but it was in another part of the city.

Months later, while in discussions with Portuguese-speaking soldiers inside the prison, Don learned that their crime had been passing out Christian tracts on the street during Independence celebrations. None of us had any inkling that this was illegal, since we had experienced much freedom of religious expression during the time of the provisional government. Previously, under the Portuguese government, all public Protestant religious activities outside the church buildings had been forbidden.

The church development process that had been ongoing for several years had to be sped up. The Lord provided the impetus to begin the turning over of authority by the mission to the Mozambican national church, especially matters relating to the division of mission and church funds. The selection of national leaders and election of governing bodies became a high priority. Long and difficult discussions took up much of the meeting time of the executive committee and mission council. Media coverage of government plans to nationalize mission properties showed the necessity of speeding up the process of turning over leadership for the clinic, day school, and Bible school, as well as mission housing and finances.

Issues that arose from the loss of security and families leaving the country were very discouraging, but it could have been worse. Portuguese-speaking Christians arrived from other congregations and joined in the life of our church. They brought encouragement through their attendance and giving. Their churches had been closed as their leaders fled the country under threat for cooperating with the previous government. Many of those who left couldn't handle the constant uncertainty of new political and economic realities. When the new government nationalized all housing, many lost their life savings. Schools became a place of frequent political meetings rather than a place of preparation for life's work or general enrichment.

Most families headed to Portugal, where they had maintained ties through generations, even while living in Mozambique. One such family was that of Manuel Reis. Word reached us later that he and his family became heavily involved in the development of the Church of the Nazarene there. Others found new homes among the Portuguese living in the Republic of South Africa, while others looked to Brazil for the opportunity to start a new life. The Newman Smith family went to Brazil. She had been a guard in the women's prison, which was part of the complex that also included the men's prison. She did her best to serve as a means of communication between prisoners and their families until they moved.

In February before Independence, the provisional government announced the official name change of the capital, from Lourenço Marques to Maputo. Soon the process of changing the names of suburbs, streets, and cities throughout the country followed.

6
Arrest and Imprisonment

A few days before Independence celebrations, a group of missionary and national leaders gathered in a private home in Maputo to finalize details for an upcoming evangelistic event that was to be held in the bull ring. For some reason, this event was not planned in cooperation with the Christian Council, and as a result, it was viewed by the political authorities as being politically inspired. They felt insurrection was the goal.

Pauline Doll had returned to the United States on August 17, 1975, to be with her mother who was experiencing major health problems. Armand planned to join her in a few weeks. He was organizing details for Frank Howie to take up responsibilities as field director upon his and Heather's return from home assignment.

On Thursday afternoon August 28, a knock came at the Dolls' door, and Armand was arrested. The police emptied filing cabinets and turned furnishings upside down as a thorough search was made of their home. Later discussions revealed that the police had suspected him of obtaining the apartment to spy on FRELIMO party offices in the building. This would have been a rather amazing feat since it had been rented years earlier for a newly arriving missionary couple, the Kanises, and later used by the Dolls.

A search followed at Armand's field office across town. They found cassette tape playback machines, a sewing machine, Bible study books and pamphlets, and a microphone. These were photographed and confiscated as evidence that the Nazarene missionaries were involved in espionage against the Mozambican people. The judiciary police later posted pictures of this display in an article in the official newspaper, the *Noticias*. Official announcements for FRELIMO were made in this way.

We were very angry and frustrated because there was no opportunity for explanations or rebuttals. The police didn't know, and we never got to say, that the cassette players provided pre-recorded sermons and Bible studies in the Shangaan language for pastors and church leaders. We never had a trial, only this public condemnation.

That afternoon we were planning to invite Armand for the evening meal at our apartment. Evelyn had gone to a nearby house where Assembly of God missionaries Dave and Jan Hall were living, while Gayla, Michael, and I headed up the elevator to invite "Uncle" Armand to dinner.

(Missionary children often treated missionary adults with familial names.) Upon arriving, we were surprised to be greeted by an unknown person speaking English. It was obvious that something very unusual was happening. Armand tried quietly to signal us that we should leave. A policeman told us to be seated, and he wrote down my name and other pertinent contact information before we were allowed to go—without Armand.

For months, we had had premonitions that something was about to happen and now, suddenly, it was upon us. We feared that lies and rumors would cause the Mozambicans to lose confidence in us. The Mozambican church's participation in giving to the worldwide evangelism endeavors might be construed as lack of loyalty to Mozambique. There were rumors circulated that church funds were illegally being sent out of the country. The Mozambique church received far more financial support from beyond the borders than any amount the church might have donated to global causes. Questions were swirling. We had no idea how it would happen or when, but suddenly, possibilities had become reality.

Later it was discovered that a government clampdown (in the form of arrests and questionings) on the Church of the Nazarene mission leadership had been planned for some time.

We arranged with the Halls to keep an eye on the Doll apartment building through the night so we could trace Armand's movements. We tried to notify the officials at the US Consulate, but I'm not sure we had the presence of mind to notify the Nazarene World Mission Department. We didn't even know if Armand was actually under arrest or what was happening. Needless to say, we didn't get much sleep that night.

In the morning, we decided that I should return to the Dolls' apartment since I had been the one who earlier had contact with the police agents. The Halls reported that lights had been on all night, and it appeared that someone was still there. We wanted to learn from the guards what we could about Armand. When I arrived at the door, I found two policemen in the apartment, as well as André Chilengue, the Nazarene high school student who worked for the Dolls in exchange for their paying his school fees. The police didn't know where Armand was, but thought he was under arrest. They allowed André to go to the shop on the ground floor of the building to buy bread for their morning tea. Since they had allowed André to go, it seemed possible that I would also be allowed to go—that I was not under arrest—so I left for home.

Because so many things happened that day, I am uncertain about the order of events, but I know that Senhora Newman Smith, the guard in the women's prison, got a message to us that Armand had indeed been arrested and placed in the Central Prison nearby. He needed several things such as his Bible, his toothbrush, and a pair of pajamas. She also reported that the police were now looking for me. We needed to get word to Lorraine Schultz and Pat Buffet at the mission station in Tavane to let them know to leave the country by side roads and not through the city, since the police were arresting women as well as men for questioning or detention.

An interview conducted by David Martin, a journalist for the *Observer,* wrote an article published in *Noticias,* highlighting the danger to women during these days:

Martin: The BBC news and other means of communication made reference to forced labor on a grand scale, political repression, and concentration camps in Mozambique. Could you give some thoughts on these issues?

Samora Machel: In the first place, since the creation of the new Republic, we have closed prisons, not opened new prisons. Besides this we are destroying the concentration camps, called "strategic villages" and have freed a million and a half Mozambicans. They were living in concentration camps and were being brutalized. Now we have in prison the scourings created by colonialism—drug users, thieves, prostitutes, criminal elements, smugglers, etc....

We learned that when the authorities found unaccompanied women, their status was immediately changed to that of "prostitute," and they were imprisoned. As a result, we were eager to get the women missionaries out of the country.

Evelyn rounded up the things Armand had asked for that morning, and we decided to ask Mrs. Smith to get them to him. I headed off to the US Consulate where I spoke with Jim Overly, the official who had checked on us before Independence. He had visited US and Canadian dependents living in the country. The conversation included the recently arrived *chargé de affairs,* Johnnie Carson, who was preparing the consulate for becoming an embassy.

We discussed my three options since the police were now looking for me.

First, I could go home and wait for the police to find me since they knew where we lived. After seeing the mess they had made of the Dolls' house and knowing the trauma that would put Evelyn and our children through, that didn't make sense.

Second, I could get in the car and drive immediately to the borders of Swaziland or the Republic of South Africa. This plan would leave my family stranded as Evelyn's United States driver's license had lapsed and we had only the one vehicle.

Third, I could go to the office of the state security police to learn why they were looking for me and answer their concerns. This seemed to make the most sense since I believed I had not disobeyed any laws. After letting Evelyn and the children know what was happening, I headed to the office of the police that afternoon, August 29.

Evelyn managed to get our car keys to Eduardo Meixieira, the church's assistant pastor, to keep an eye on the car until she needed it again. I walked to the police station and explained to the police inspector who I was and why I was there. The inspector, Jorge Antunes da Costa, turned me over to an agent. The agent proceeded to question me. He seemed quite aware of who I was, the church I was pastoring, the mission team I was a part of, and various activities our church youth had been involved in during the time of the provisional government.

The agents directed me to write out a statement of our discussion that day, and then they took me from the police offices to the Central Prison, also dubbed the "Reeducation Center."

Inside the prison, I was led to the stairs just beyond the main doors. At the top was a gate where Armand was standing with other prisoners. When he recognized me, he said my name, and I acknowledged him. I was led to the other upstairs wing and placed in a large cell with other detainees. It was the coolest part of the winter, so someone found me a blanket and a place to sleep on the floor. This became the longest night of my life!

Questions swirled in my mind: Did my family know where I was? Where was God when this was happening? Did anyone care?

Stories of homosexual rape and abuse flooded through my mind. No one looked familiar—or even friendly. These people in maximum security were obviously there because they were considered dangerous, and they looked the part. In time, we came to know some of the South

Africans and ethnic Indians. They were in maximum security because they had attempted to escape, but they didn't look friendly—not that first night.

After a troubled night, the new day brought release from maximum security—perhaps it served for holding new prisoners—to the regular prison on the main floor. I made my way to the cell in block B where my friend, Don Milam, was being held. A week later when Armand was released from maximum security, he joined us. We three US missionaries shared the cell the whole time we were "guests." Other prisoners whom we knew, stayed in other parts of the prison. Two Nazarene co-workers who were members of the literature office staff, pastor Manuel Tshambe and Noé Chilengue, as well as Noé's brother André, were also arrested during this time. Don's co-workers, Clécius and Saluh, while housed elsewhere, often came to our cell to eat.

We made a special plea to the authorities to allow Evelyn to visit me. Two days later, she was let in, and we had our first visit. On September 1, during visiting hours, she brought Gayla and Mike to see me. It helped the children to visualize where I was and why I was not with them at home. This was the last time I would see any of them for eight months.

The following day, I was taken back to the office of the judiciary police for questioning. It was for further clarifications on my original statement. The man in charge of the office where I had been taken claimed he was not part of the police but was a representative of the justice department. He was a sympathetic member of the Methodist Church who spoke of his belief in God, though veiled in quotations about nature. I never saw him again. It could be that he and the police agent were playing the "good cop/bad cop" game. Later, other prisoners told me I shouldn't have signed the statement, but since it was obviously in my handwriting, I had signed it.

The United States vice consul went to our apartment the next day, and while he was there, Lorraine Schultz and Pat Buffet arrived from the Tavane mission station. They had heard that Armand had been arrested but were unaware of my imprisonment. At that point, all the Nazarene missionaries remaining in the country and not in prison were at our apartment. Once the vice consul realized this, he directed them—the three ladies and two children—to leave the country as soon as possible because the consulate couldn't guarantee their safety.

Evelyn had a couple of hours to find the little blue Volkswagen, pack up our life, and leave for South Africa. She took care of all the final details, trying not to forget anything. It was hard for her to concentrate. How could she abandon her husband? The prison walls already brought separation, but now it would be miles. What a blessing that she would have support from the ladies who were leaving with her.

A break from the mounting tension came from an unexpected place. Along the highway at one of the security stops, a soldier propped his AK-47 against the car as he searched. Everyone in the car had to exit while the search took place. Michael, an inquisitive two-year-old, decided to investigate the machine gun, but his mother caught him before any harm was done. As they neared the border, they noticed that a plane was circling over the border post, and they feared that messages were being radioed to the border authorities to stop them from leaving the country. But with much prayer, they went through the border-crossing procedures and were allowed to leave with no more difficulty than usual.

An event two months prior to my imprisonment proved providential on this August day. Pat had agreed to take my family to Nelspruit, the nearest town in South Africa, for dental appointments. We had filled out paperwork for her to be allowed to drive our VW across the border. Little did we know that the earlier permission made it possible to get the ladies and the children out of the country in safety. In addition, they had transportation for the months they were in South Africa. Evelyn was able to sell it just before she left for the US.

We got news about what was going on during visiting hours on the Wednesday they left when Cape Verdean friend and parishioner Domingo Rodrigues came to see us. Another friend, Allen (Hélio), entered for a short visit to explain that Evelyn, the kids, Pat, and Lorraine had left for South Africa. It had been reported that all Nazarene missionaries were to be questioned by the police, hence the need for their immediate departure. This was bittersweet news. Their safety was paramount but now the long separation had begun.

After waiting and wondering if they had made it safely across the border, I finally received Evelyn's first letter on September 23. What a great day of rejoicing to hear that she and the children had arrived in South Africa safely and were well! However, Evelyn told how Michael would occasionally walk around the house where they were staying and call out my name, wondering where I was. (I had to destroy that letter and all the others I received in case there was a raid on the cells by the guards or soldiers who might question how I had received them. They arrived via "visitor delivery" not through the administrator's office.)

I made my last visit to the office of the judiciary police on the fifth of September. During this nearly all-day affair, I was accused of being anti-communist. I was questioned about items in Armand's office, including a lapel microphone. When I tried to figure out what the agent was talking about, hesitating in the process, he accused me of lying. It was one of the most frustrating experiences I had ever been through! I was given the file which included the charges being brought against me ("suspicion of anti-state activities") to review for a few minutes. I was the only one of the three from the US who had any idea at that time what the charges against us were, yet none of us was taken before our accusers in court.

During my questioning, of particular interest to the agents was the poster that had been distributed at Easter. It was a drawing of Jesus on the cross, with the words (in Portuguese): "Father, forgive them, for they do not know what they are doing" (Luke 24:34 NIV). The agent pointed out that he saw the message to be a statement of criticism of the new government rather than the evangelistic message we intended it to have. Under the Portuguese regime, the church had to hold all activities within the walls of the church building, but during the time of transition, we felt more freedom since the new constitution provided for religious freedom. A team from YWAM (Youth with a Mission) South Africa had come in May for three days of ministry, holding music concerts in local parks. They reached out in a public way by holding concerts and distributing tracts and posters. Other than attracting the attention of the officials, we didn't see any response from this campaign.

Hugh, Armand, Don and Clécius

7
Day in the Life

Though we had no idea how long we were going to be in the prison, we quickly developed a regular daily pattern. At the beginning, we would get up early, shower and shave and get dressed as nicely as we could. We would then have a cup of coffee and some bread. We were always ready in case we were called back to the judiciary police offices, hoping to clarify our statements in order to obtain our release.

After we did morning clean-up, we had visitors from inside the prison much of the day. The prisoners brought their cups and instant coffee or tea to our cell because we had one of the few electric kettles. Some came and spent time talking; others came only to get hot water. Once the prisoners found there were three "priests" in the prison, we had many opportunities to hear their stories and problems. One story that affected me deeply was of a wife struggling to feed the family with her husband in prison. She turned to prostitution because of the lack of work. He was devastated.

Before Armand and I arrived, Don and Clécius, his co-worker, led several young men to faith in Jesus. They had been bouncers in the nightclubs downtown near the docks.

They were released or expelled from the country not long afterwards.

Each cell was about six by twelve feet with high ceilings which later helped us cope with the heat. Opposite the heavy wooden door was the only window, with metal bars, torn screen, and broken glass.

Mosquitos were a real problem. Armand was constantly working to patch the screens to protect us from the malaria-infected pests. We were glad someone thought to send anti-malaria drugs.

But the presence of mosquitos also had its lighter side. One night a lone mosquito was buzzing around, and no one was sleeping well. Tony began throwing his pillow into the air trying to knock it down. We all woke up fully and joined the fray with lots of laughter.

There were two metal bunkbeds in the cell and one single bed. The beds had metal springs and old "sponge" mattresses which were very dirty and uncomfortable and didn't give good support. A built-in table, where the electric kettle and a hot plate were kept, stood in the corner.

We usually had five people in the cell. In addition to Armand, Don, and me, for quite a long period, first José (Zé) and then António (Tony) occupied the fourth bed. Tony worked for the national bus service as the head mechanic. He suspected he had been arrested because the buses kept breaking down. His thought was that these were caused by both the lack of training of the drivers and the horrible state of the roads. He was accused of economic sabotage.

The person in the fifth position, occupying the bed above me, changed more often. I have no clear memories of the names of these men. I think our use of Portuguese and English was confusing to them, and they spent very little time in the cell except to sleep.

We three from the US liked fresh air in the cell; our African and Portuguese cellmates had different ideas, especially at night. It was a constant point of contention between us.

Since this was a very old building with no electric outlets in the cells, creative prisoners had rigged up connections to access electricity. The electricity would occasionally blink out at night, and guards would be called to come reset the breaker. Electrical wire was also strung across the cell from the air vent above the door and attached to the bars at the window for clothes-drying. Fortunately, we never had electric shocks, but we were aware of some who did because of their obvious electrical burns.

In the time before my imprisonment, Evelyn and I were often very ill with malaria, which is endemic along coastlines in the tropics. Our apartment had screens on the windows, but we were often out walking in the grass early in the morning and late in the afternoon when malaria mosquitos were active. In prison, despite less protection, we seldom had attacks of malaria. We learned of outbreaks of typhoid and cholera in the city and thanked the Lord that, even in such crowded and unsanitary conditions, the prison population was unaffected.

At one point, I believe I tried to pass a kidney stone. I was in intense pain but had no readily available medical care. I talked to the "doctor" —one of the South Africans who claimed to be one—and he thought it was just back pain from sleeping on the poor-quality beds. There were also occasional problems with toothaches and headaches, but we were amazingly free of medical problems.

Sundays were usually celebrated as a special day. At the beginning, we were able to use the chapel for evangelical Christian services. Because it was designed and built as a Roman Catholic worship space, there were priest's vestments in a storeroom, and a confessional booth. Prisoners would occasionally get into the building at unauthorized times. One day a person was seen running around the prison yard wearing the priest's robe, which greatly offended the Roman Catholic prisoners. Then the confessional booth was taken out into the exercise and visitors' yard where it was used as an outdoor urinal because there was no facility for prisoners or guests to use during their time outdoors. More offense! When we saw that it had been carried over and placed against the outside wall, we were not surprised when some prisoners used it to crawl over the wall during the night.

Prisoners who escaped were quickly caught and severely beaten. Probably ten or so prisoners attempted to escape during our time but as far as I know, all were caught, returned to the prison, and punished.

From time to time the prisoner responsible for our cell block (*chef da aula*) would bring additional inmates. One time we had to make room for a group of 35 Jehovah's Witnesses. (They were part of a group that turned themselves in to the authorities because they were being publicly accused of disloyalty. They wouldn't salute and proclaim *"Viva, FRELIMO"* at political rallies or serve in the military). We had fascinating discussions with those assigned to sleep in our small cell. They were with us a few weeks before they were shipped off to work camps. Reports were circulated stating that as many as 180 Jehovah's Witnesses had been imprisoned.

Other "guests" came, too. A group of Rhodesians captured in a cross-border raid were imprisoned. They were railway workers and were released quickly.

Two others arrested, Klaus and Giovanni, representing the European Economic Union, were negotiating with the Mozambican government for the purchase of fruit to export to Europe. They had been invited by a department of the government. Klaus took lots of pictures and recorded his observations on tape. This obviously attracted the attention of the authorities. They were arrested at their luxurious hotel, the Polana, and brought to the other "Polana Hotel," (which was our nickname for the Central Prison). We helped by sharing our food and talking with them. They were interesting fellows who were discernibly frustrated at the lack of cooperation between government departments.

CHAPEL - LOURENÇO MARQUES
PENITENCIARY

One Sunday we discovered a pump organ, which Armand played. The following Sunday our numbers swelled and so did our voices.

It was a sad day when we were no longer allowed to use the chapel. This ban occurred in October in conjunction with the all-prison search and removal of books and Bibles. Prisoners were prohibited from singing Christian songs together in the cells. We continued having private devotions, but we were always careful because of potential spies. In fact, one prisoner told us that he had been approached by the authorities to spy on us. From that time on, we avoided drawing unnecessary attention to ourselves by having group meetings or leaving the New Testament where it could be seen.

****

On Sunday evenings, many prisoners gathered in the rotunda to mingle with prisoners from other parts of the prison. From time to time, we would have "movie night," the movies usually coming from a local theater. The owner was a prisoner, and another inmate was a projectionist. Most of the time the movies were in English or French with Portuguese sub-titles.

When Sunday visitation hour was over, I would stand at the gate that faced toward our apartment. This was the time my congregation was gathering for their main public service of the week. My heart was heavy, as I deeply missed my family and my people.

****

Besides reading and talking with prisoners and visitors, other activities occupied our time. I really enjoyed playing chess even though I held the bottom position in the chess tournaments. While interest waned from time to time, we played regularly until our release.

Other games played in the prison were Checkers and an African version of Mancala. The players moved the stones around in cup-shaped holes and got rather excited about it, sometimes even gambling on the outcome. There would be two or three of those games set up and being played when we were outside in the recreation area. I also saw a game that reminded me of a combination of Checkers and Sorry, which had a homemade board with lines and circles drawn on it and was played with bottle caps.

Some of us passed time by doing exercises, often early in the morning or after check-in at night. That way we would avoid the mass of people looking on. Tony had a hand weight (dumbbell) which he left with us upon his release. The Rhodesians who were with us for a while got us doing very vigorous exercises at night. One Hindu prisoner was a yoga master. He encouraged us to try workouts which would have less visible results but would last longer. He also encouraged us to avoid the direct sunlight during our outdoor breaks. We were spending time sunbathing, and he felt that was harmful. I proved him right a few times by unwise over-exposure, getting bad burns.

Many of us celebrated our birthdays during our imprisonment, and Armand usually prepared something special on those days, like his "hot plate cookies." Don and I were only in our thirties, so we had a most notable celebration when Armand turned sixty.

We were responsible for keeping our own cells clean, and usually on Tuesday mornings we would clean everything and wash the floors. Then about every twenty days we were assigned to hall and bathroom clean-up duty which lasted about two hours. From time to time, we joined the cleaning crew at 4:30 in the morning. Our job was to remove the trash from the cell blocks to the street in front of the prison. Even this little taste of freedom was precious, and the temptation to try to escape was always present. But remembering the vicious beatings of all re-captured prisoners deterred those thoughts. The only time it even seemed possible was when I took the garbage out to the side of the prison building, which put me within sight of our apartment. But even then, there was a soldier within eyeshot and my family wasn't there anymore.

Occasionally, Don and I were assigned to work on the crew cleaning up leaves, grass, and trash from where the visitors entered the prison. Most of the time the guards and soldiers used this area. I helped clean the soldiers' cells and their eating area, where they threw chicken bones and other trash from their meals.

Our cleaning equipment consisted of worn-out blankets that we dragged along the cement. No disinfectant, soap, or detergent. But there was so little that was worthwhile to do in the prison that we were thankful to be a part of even these clean-up crews.

Just as we cleaned our cell and the surrounding prison areas, we also needed personal hygiene. Among the foreign prisoners was a South African, Owen Greenwood, a convert to Islam who was skilled at cutting hair. We called him by his chosen name, Sharif. We were thankful that he was willing to keep us looking neat. There were also barbers among the African prisoners who cared for the majority of inmates. Evelyn sent hygiene items into the prison early on for us including nail clippers, razors, bath towels, and wash cloths.

The reader has perhaps noticed that I haven't mentioned any sanitation facilities in our cell. Usually, we had the run of the cell block day and night. The bathing and toilet facilities available to us were at the far end of the cell block from the rotunda. This is also where we washed up our dishes and silverware. Many of the men in the prison had never been in a restroom before, so the conditions were very unsanitary.

A lack of water was a problem in the city, but we only had one week when we didn't have any on the inside. In addition, we were amazed that the water didn't make us sick. Thanks be to God for the prayers of God's people, and his continuing protection!

Occasionally, the lights would go out, the radio that was in our cell would go silent, and the soldiers locked us in our cells. We would find out later that there had been some kind of visit by a dignitary such as Julius Nyerere, president of Tanzania (which occurred in August), or Kenneth Kaunda, president of Zambia (in April). Or it might be the celebration of another socialist country's independence, such as Angola (November 11) and Tanzania (December 9).

It might be related to a crisis, like the time on December 17 when, during an attempted coup by Makhuwa and Makonde soldiers from northern Mozambique, the president's life was threatened. We learned very little about these incidents in the official media but heard the details from our visitors. It was said that the soldiers from the north of Mozambique were unhappy that the southern tribes had control of the government and decided to launch a counter-revolution. Their attempt was put down quickly, but it made us feel very exposed. It was reported that the vice-commandant of the soldiers assigned to prison security was being transferred, but later it became obvious he had been involved in the attempted coup.

The official news agency repeatedly reported that everything in the country was running well. We were careful not to refer to specific national matters. We didn't pass on anything we heard. Often, by the time our families got the news of a crisis it had passed, but they feared we were still in immediate danger.

Another important aspect of life in prison was maintaining the balance between soldiers, guards, and prisoners because each group had a certain amount of power.

The guards were employees of the state and were under the prison administrator. Since many had worked under the Portuguese government and had experience with how prisons operated, they tended to be sympathetic to the prisoners' situation.

The soldiers were under the military authority in the persons of a commandant and his assistant. They carried machine guns, and it didn't help that many didn't speak or understand Portuguese or Shangaan. Their tactics were often quite brutal.

The prisoners, surprisingly, had means of communication with individuals in positions of national authority, and would occasionally report abuses. These reports, however, could have repercussions by way of mistreatment perpetrated by the soldiers and the vice-commandant.

In November, a group of eighty (mostly foreign) prisoners signed a complaint regarding the treatment of prisoners, including the torture of the cell block leaders. One copy was smuggled out of the prison addressed to the country's president. Another was turned over to the director and the commandant, along with a futile request to pass it on to higher-ups. That November day began a week of terror!

Don, Armand, and I were among the signers of the document, and were called to a "commission of denunciation" in the rotunda. We were called derogatory names, including "Boers," "Zionists" and "reactionaries" and other names they made up. We were also threatened with bodily harm.

After this harassment, the ones who called the meeting gave the cheer which all loyal Mozambicans were to answer with upraised fists and shouting, "*Viva, FRELIMO.*" None of us responded.

The following Tuesday, the signers were called to the chapel building, but nothing happened. Later we were called to a meeting with the commandant, who told us that the vice-commandant, Fernando, had been punished. Our punishment was that there would be no visits and no time outside.

On the following day, at about 8:00 am, we were again called together. The commandant announced that visits had been reinstated and that we needed to sign a declaration explaining why we had signed the complaint addressed to the president. An hour later we had a meeting with the prison director. He told us that for some reason, the visits for the Jehovah's Witness prisoners had also been okayed. Most of us were not aware they had been revoked. At 10:00 am, the soldiers took away the hot plates from the cells, but they were returned at 11:00. It was a very uncertain and unsettling time.

From time to time, we would become aware that some prisoners enjoyed special privileges, and we always suspected that gifts had been given. Some prisoners had managed to escape, and the talk was that bribes had been paid by family or friends. One Indian prisoner spent a day outside the prison at the time of the Hindu religious festival, Diwali. Yet at the end of the day he returned, which was very puzzling.

8
Inmates and Visitors

In the early days of my incarceration, I tried to familiarize myself with the facility layout. In the central area of the prison, three wings met together at a rotunda with a hallway that led to a gate at the street. Along this hallway were the offices and quarters of the guards and soldiers and the storerooms used to hold personal items which had been confiscated from the prisoners. The gate was where prisoners would stand before mealtimes, hoping for a glimpse of the familiar face of someone bringing food.

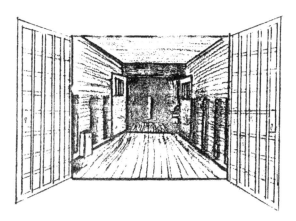

Inner gates of the Prison

Outside another set of rotunda gates, there was access to the outdoor visiting area, the chapel, and the place where we did our laundry. When we had visitors, we would place benches from our cells under the trees that lined the edge of the visiting area.

On the other side of the main building was a soccer field, a cement structure originally built for maintenance of prison vehicles, several guard houses, and the prison chapel. Before our confinement, a Roman Catholic priest came to the chapel to say mass for the prisoners. With his departure we found joy in keeping it open and operating until we were no longer allowed to use it.

Outside another prison door was a much smaller outdoor exercise and resting area, and a shop. At one time, the workshop had been open to the prisoners, but when they began to use the tools to create weapons or means of escape, the shop was closed and therefore it was unavailable by the time we arrived. An unused entrance to the women's part of the prison was located a short distance away.

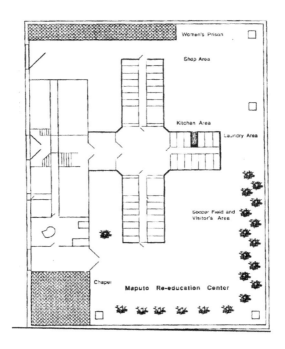

Prison Overview

Visitors usually came for a couple of hours two to three times a week. Those who had lined up at the front sidewalk would pass through security, submit their identification documents, and then enter the meeting area. At first, all prisoners could receive visitors every visiting day; however, after the numbers in the prison climbed to 500, there was neither room nor security personnel for so many at once. Visitation was cut back to once or twice a week. And even that schedule was interrupted at times expected to attend special events at the national stadium.

Having visitors was normally an exciting time. We would hear about family, church members, and what was happening on the street. However, having visitors also had its downside as they shared their problems and stresses with us. We often ended up discouraged by the time they left.

Visiting hours were also times when we would pass messages written to our families. These would later be mailed or carried to neighboring countries. We received many of our notes the same way, although many came hidden in food or supplies, including toilet paper, and other personal items brought in at mealtimes. Messages written on—or rolled up in—toilet paper rolls became a common means of communication.

For a time, our wives visited. Evelyn came twice before she was instructed to leave the country. Don's wife, Micki, came often before leaving Mozambique, but it was difficult for their children to come.

In late September, Micki arrived visibly shaken. She had made a deal to sell their furniture as she was getting ready to move into the Halls' place since they were leaving the country. She was awakened during the night, and when she went downstairs to investigate the noise, she saw a man carrying out a final load of her furniture. When she screamed, the thieves jumped into the truck and quickly drove off.

She filed a report with the police who wanted more information about her as the victim than about what was taken or any clues as to who might have committed the robbery. She returned the money to the people who had purchased the furniture and waited. A few weeks later, Micki received word that the furniture had been found. She got the pieces back to the buyers, re-collected the money, and moved to the Halls' house. Their home had a telephone, which was a lot more convenient for Micki to keep in contact with friends and family outside the country.

****

One day, when we were enjoying our free time outside, a prisoner from South Africa, Kimo, attacked a soldier. Suddenly everything stopped. Holding our breaths, we watched to see what would happen. All the soldiers were called, and we were afraid they would begin firing their weapons. Instead, Kimo was captured and taken to the isolation cell in block C.

Early the next Thursday morning, about 2:30, we heard Kimo making noise and singing, trying to attract attention. This was the beginning of what appeared to be insanity. About 4:15 pm the following Friday, during visiting hours, while one of the other cell blocks was out in the visiting area, Kimo was brought out from the disciplinary cell to get some air and use the toilet.

When I saw Kimo walking around freely, I thought about going over to him because during the first few months, we had spent many hours talking together. But I felt a check and stood watching him across the rotunda. Suddenly, he tried to grab a soldier's rifle. The soldiers had been told not to carry rifles within the prison, yet here was an AK-47. The soldier lifted his gun and shot him! The bullet went through Kimo's stomach and out the other side, ricocheting off the floor and wall, just missing the large gathering of people in the rotunda.

He lay in his blood until the commandant ordered prisoners to carry him to the front gate from where he was transported to the city hospital. We spent an hour that evening in a meeting with the commandant in an effort to cool us all down. On the following Tuesday, we received word that Kimo was out of danger.

Two weeks later, he was returned to the prison, but was placed in solitary confinement where we could have very limited contact with him. After a few days, he was allowed out of the disciplinary cell and seemed to be okay. From this point on until my release, he kept to himself, though I did have a few opportunities to encourage him.

When prisoners tried to escape, we understood their longing for freedom, but it meant reprisals for the rest of us. One attempt led to a lockdown in our cell blocks. Soldiers came and rounded up the three *chefs da aula*. After being beaten, they were taken into the rotunda where their elbows were tied together behind their backs with hemp rope. Salt was poured on the wounds, and they were left to scream for hours. We all suffered with them.

One FRELIMO soldier seemed to take a liking to Armand and another to Tony. For several weeks, they came in the evenings to visit them in our cell. They spoke rather openly about the situation in the country and their assignments. One had been on patrol on the border of Swaziland and talked about tracking people down who were trying to escape. He couldn't understand why people wanted out of Mozambique and decided they must be criminals. While Tony enjoyed leading them on, the rest of us were nervous having soldiers in our cell, especially when they stayed for so long and came close to criticizing the government.

Life in the prison brought many unexpected turns. But a key to survival resulted from relationships built on the inside as well as with those who visited.

Outside of the Prison

9
Living with the Uncertainties

As was noted previously, when Evelyn and I were appointed to Mozambique, we had little clue of what was happening in the country. That some were fighting a war for independence from Portugal in the north of the country was unknown to us. With little background or previous knowledge, what we learned from our research at the library was not particularly alarming. The country of Mozambique was large, and the struggle seemed to be localized in the north, far from the capital, where we thought the mission council would appoint us.

When we arrived in Portugal, we focused on learning the Portuguese language and culture. Plus, we had an infant, so we paid little attention to political matters in Mozambique. Reading *Time* magazine didn't provide much helpful information.

Most of our contacts from within Portugal were from Cape Verde or were part of the ex-pat community—people away from their home countries. Many were in language study and were soon heading for various parts of the

Portuguese Empire. We learned little from them about what was happening in Mozambique.

Even after we arrived, we were not confronted with the realities of the struggle along the Tanzanian border in the north. By then, I was able to read the newspaper in Portuguese, but the duties to which we were assigned, our son's birth, and getting settled in another country and culture, prevented me from paying much attention to far-away disturbances. Most who were aware took the attitude, "It can't happen here."

In the April 1974 Revolution of the Carnations, Portugal moved toward socialism. We knew there was discontent among many Portuguese, but not to the extent of a revolution! Because we hadn't paid close enough attention to the political situation, this caught us off guard, and we needed to quickly learn background and repercussions. Caetano was dictator of Portugal in the years Evelyn and I were in Europe. Now he was being ousted, and a socialist regime took control.

It was a time of rapid and disorienting change. When we were imprisoned, we needed to face some realities. The "realities" of which I speak included:

- What would life look like for the church and the mission under socialism and possibly totalitarian communism?

- Under this regime, things were not as they had been for the church in Mozambique. What would the situation look like in the future?

- Would US and other Western missionaries be allowed to stay?

- Would the national Nazarene church be folded up into a National Church of Mozambique, which might even include Muslims, as we had heard rumored?

- Would Mozambican Nazarenes be allowed to freely operate since the Church of the Nazarene was assumed to be anti-Communist?

The deep sense of frustration of the African Mozambicans, the bewilderment on the part of our Portuguese congregation and friends, and our questions about what God might be doing, brought on confusion and unrest.

An ongoing internal struggle throughout this imprisonment experience had to do with its purpose or meaning. How did this experience fit into God's calling on our lives and the development of the church in Mozambique?

The Lord at Work

Even in our discouragement and lack of understanding, things were moving outside the prison. Over the years, the Lord had enabled the mission organization of the church to work effectively, and a strong church had been established under missionary and national leadership. When the missionaries left, the Mozambican church carried on their own effective program. Word reached us in prison that the church felt we were being more helpful to them through our imprisonment than during our time of freedom because they were compelled to lead without outside help!

For example, the Maputo Portuguese-language church, which I had been serving as pastor, learned some valuable lessons in love by ministering to our needs. They brought many of the meals, most of our toilet articles, and some items of clothing and footwear. It seemed to us that as they ministered to us, the Lord helped them to work out their differences and to sense new direction in their lives. Something happened to them as a result of having to accept different responsibilities. Many remained involved in the church when they left the country. In some cases, they became involved in planting new congregations in various places (South Africa, Portugal, and Brazil).

The Lord also had some things He wanted to accomplish in me. He let me see more fully the kind of person I am, with my strengths and weaknesses. He helped me realize what a wonderful wife and family I have. I learned lessons of patience and confidence—patience with God's timing and with friends, and confidence in Jesus and His Church.

But perhaps the most encouraging was the response of so many people in North America, who felt that they had also gained something from our incarceration. They came to realize the truth that God heard their prayers. Many learned what it means to express love and concern through praying for people they didn't know, and then seeing the Lord answer prayer. This was life-changing for many. Most of this we realized only later. In the situation itself, this reality could not be clearly seen.

****

After a month or two, we began to lose hope of getting out. We neglected to shave and dress neatly because we no longer thought we might be called to the "judiciary" police office for a hearing or for additional clarifications. It seemed the legal system only worked to get people into prison, not to get them out. We experienced many lonely and discouraging days.

September 24, we heard an announcement of the establishing of official relations between Mozambique and the United States. This caused a high level of anticipation for our release, though there was a strong sense of skepticism as well.

My diary tells me visitors regularly reported we would soon be released. I remember Dona Natercia, a former member of the church I pastored, on her October 18 visit, emphatically assuring us that everything would be worked out soon. She said we would soon be allowed to return to our families and responsibilities. We tended to treat these "predictions" as words to encourage us, with little or no basis in fact.

Radio South Africa reported on January 22 that there would "soon" be a release of Portuguese prisoners in Mozambique. On March 5, we heard a rumor that all foreigners in another of the city's prisons, the Commando Prison, were released. However, we didn't receive confirmation that this was so. Then an Indian prisoner,

Kaku, predicted that all foreigners would leave the prison before May 15, which turned out to be true in my case!

What usually happened when these rumors came was that I would have a series of vivid dreams of being at home with Evelyn and the children. That would be followed by several days of depression because we remained in prison.

In his recollections of similar situations during his imprisonment in Nazi Germany, Dietrich Bonhoeffer remarked, "I'm dreaming more and more that I have been released and am back home with you" (*Letters and Papers from Prison*). The separation from family and the congregation, as well as our work, was one of the most difficult things to deal with in prison, and one Bonhoeffer affirmed.

It took much of my imprisonment to recognize that God was indeed very active in our experience. He hadn't spared our going through the difficulties, but was with us every step of the way, though we didn't always see this clearly at the time. Through the years, many have asked how we were able to handle the uncertainties and discouragement. Usually, I would answer by talking of four things: food, health, protection, and the Bible. We knew God had His hand on our situation. There was evidence in His daily care: He provided food through friends, health despite filthy conditions, safety from mistreatment, and a copy of God's Word.

Food

People bringing meals would queue up at the outside door and pass the food basket or aluminum stacked containers so common in the Portuguese world to the guards or soldiers. They would do a quick glance to make sure there were no hidden weapons or other banned items. Trusted prisoners then carried the items to the waiting prisoners. Often seeing the visitor at a distance was the only glimpse we had of these angelic messengers. Friends brought not only food but also other necessities such as toothpaste, soap, and toilet paper in this way. It was a very special treat when church leaders brought us bags of home-prepared peanuts and cashews.

When Evelyn heard that friends were traveling into Mozambique from South Africa, she would contact them and arrange for things to be brought to us. One very clear memory is of a chocolate cake she sent, protected in a Kellogg's cereal box. Between the layers, she had secreted a note with personal news, and reminding us that people were praying for us. The delicious chocolate cake was much appreciated.

We received many meals from friends, missionaries of other missions and, occasionally, even from members of the US Consulate staff. As important as the daily provision of food was, the sense of not being forgotten spoke very loudly to us. The contact by these messengers reminded us that we were not alone.

Often, friends brought a special meal on Sundays, and we usually had visitors in the afternoon. Receiving food and visits on a regular basis from family and friends was a real blessing. At first that may seem like a normal, even mundane, provision. But when days stretched into weeks and weeks into months, and we continued to receive food daily from those on the outside, we recognized God's hand.

Prisoners who didn't have provisions from the outside were fed from a central kitchen somewhere in the city. Prison meals consisted of bread and tea in the morning, and mielie meal porridge with sauce at midday. Though sufficient for nutrition, we were not accustomed to this kind of menu, so were grateful for food from our friends outside the prison.

Some of our friends would prepare a meal and then walk to the bus stop or catch a taxi to come and stand for an hour or more in order to hand over the items in the basket to the guards. After spending several hours of their time to take care of us, these ministering angels would return home the same way. We were not aware if there was an organized effort to see that we five prisoners had food, but virtually every day something arrived for us to enjoy. God's message remained clear— "I know where you are, and I care, through my people!"

Health

Though Armand's health had remained stable throughout the ordeal, he was still thirty years older than we were and nearing retirement. We were healthy! The prison was very crowded and became more and more so as time passed. We counted about five hundred in cells that could accommodate maybe two hundred prisoners in bunks. Many slept on mats on the floor. No cleaning supplies were provided except one time when disinfectant was distributed by the authorities. And there was the never-ending problem of inadequate protection from mosquitos. Except for a few unusual occasions, we had clean water for personal hygiene and to do a surface cleaning of our living space. We were aware that God was watching out for our health.

But in addition to our physical health, there were also mental health issues to address. Friends and parishioners, such as Senhora Gouveia, a neighbor of the Alexanders, took care of the personal possessions of the Alexanders as well as ours. Imagine my surprise one day in October to be called to the front gate to receive a box containing a collection of books and personal items of a sentimental nature. Having these things was a great encouragement, a tangible reminder of my family. Other items in the house were sold, given away, and otherwise discarded rather than letting the authorities confiscate them. The Dolls and Howies had lost everything. The proceeds of the sale of our furniture and appliances went to finance the Smiths' move to Brazil, which made me feel we were still able to contribute to others.

A major spiritual lift came on December 15, when searching for a station brought us the voice of Jorge de Barros on *"A Hora Nazarena."* This broadcast of "The Nazarene Hour" of the Church of the Nazarene was beamed regularly into Mozambique from Trans World Radio in Swaziland, but this was the only time we ever picked it up.

What a Christmas present the message and songs brought us to encourage our hearts.

Evelyn was alert to our need for encouragement. Every message she sent to us through friends let us know that people were praying for us. She and my parents both tried to phone the prison, Evelyn to let me know that she had made it safely back to the United States, and my parents to find out if we were well. The attempts to reach us were unsuccessful, but the prison director informed us of the calls.

Safety

We thought often of our need for protection. Previously, I mentioned the beating and torture of our cell block leaders and the shooting of a prisoner. These were not the only instances when prisoners were mistreated. Occasionally, the authorities would gather the prisoners in the rotunda where we would be "educated" on the benefits of the Marxist-Leninist way of life, the glories of the struggle against fascism, Zionism, and free-market capitalism as well as the evils of the South African, Israeli, and US regimes. However, we were not subjected to extreme forms of mind and behavioral control experienced in other parts of the totalitarian world. We were very aware that being considered enemies of the people and treated as prisoners without due process of law was its own form of mistreatment. Little of our lives and experiences were considered of value.

The most terrifying time of the week was the weekend nights when the soldiers would return late from drinking. They would slam the large metal doors and, knowing the prison director and the commandant were not in the building, would often give voice to their frustrations. We always knew violence could erupt, and we relied on God's care.

The Word

Prisoners began asking for Bibles in their home languages. Visitors brought them in a variety of languages—English, Afrikaans, SiSwati, Swahili, French, Shangaan, and Portuguese—and soon there were many Bibles in the prison. This activity must have come to the attention of the prison authorities because on October 23, we were locked in our cells while a search was made. In the raid, the soldiers and prison director picked up nearly all books, along with New Testaments and Bibles.

The guards looked through my small box of photos and remembrances from home. It was a concerning moment as it also contained a New Testament. Much to our delight they left it all. For many months, this was the only copy of the Bible we had. During the raid we were promised "revolutionary" reading materials, which didn't arrive. Gradually "non-revolutionary" fiction books began to reappear.

Evelyn and some other friends would find appropriate scripture to smuggle into us. Others would send references in cards and letters. These were encouraging. I had no idea how many prisoners and prison experiences were in the Bible until I was involved in this.

Remembering that the One who called us would also bring his plans for our lives to completion (Philippians 1:6) was a mainstay for us. It helped us keep our equilibrium and was a source of hope that all this would come to an end.

A little humor also helped restore us when our moods became grim. Armand's creativity in making chocolate chip cookies on a hotplate, as well as toasted cheese sandwiches with a stinky cheese helped make life bearable.

There is One who knows how to make promises and keep them! I had sure evidence of this in Jesus' words, my life verse: "I myself will be with you every day until the end of this present age" (Matthew 28:20, CEV). As much as I might have liked it, the promise is not that He would keep me out of trouble, but that He would be with me in every situation.

It was significant that we three from the US were able to be cellmates, which provided an opportunity for us to keep close attention to each other's physical health and emotional well-being. The overarching evidence of God's care and presence was made clear in the knowledge of God's people supporting us in prayer.

10
Release—Free at Last!

In his reading one day, Don found a statement from South African Dutch Reformed pastor Andrew Murray. Don translated it from English into Portuguese, printed it up neatly, and posted it prominently in the cell in both languages. Sweetened condensed milk is very much like Elmer's glue; it works well for sticking things on plastered walls. The downside is that cockroaches really like sweetened condensed milk.

Murray's comment, written in the early 1900s was as follows:

I Just Want to Say that I am here
By the will of God
Being kept by Him
Under His discipline
For the time he desires

Prisoners saw the statement and asked us about it. For most, it seemed hopelessly optimistic and unrealistic. But others received encouragement to hold on just one more day, as did we.

Because we were unaware of what was transpiring regarding our legal cases and release, we tended to think nothing was going on. This led to frustration and depression. We tried to deal with low spirits in three ways: remembering what God was doing on our behalf (the food, health, security, and the Bible), depending on each other, and the constant awareness that people were praying for us.

Evelyn, the two children, and our colleague Pat Buffet spent most of the eight months I was in prison in the Republic of South Africa. They stayed at Brook House Christian Workers' guest home in a suburb of Pretoria or with missionary colleagues in other South African cities. Pat had opted to stay with Evelyn to be her "secretary of transportation and encouragement." Since Evelyn had allowed her US driver's license to lapse and driving on the other side of the road with two small children was unnerving, she liked the arrangement.

As often as she could, Evelyn contacted people at the US Embassy in Pretoria, the administrative capital of South

Africa. Brook House was relatively close to the embassy. The personnel there rarely had encouraging news, but Evelyn kept reminding them of their role until the US Embassy in Maputo opened: they had responsibility for the three men from the US being held in neighboring Mozambique. She was told that US Secretary of State Henry Kissinger had made an official visit to Mozambique to pave the way for US recognition of the new republic. This included meetings dealing with our situation. Many Nazarenes and friends sent telegrams or letters to the State Department asking for our release. The US Senate appointed Willard DuPree as US ambassador and he was credentialed by the Mozambican authorities. Nazarenes and other Christians around the world urged him to focus on prompt action for our release.

****

When Pat's father became ill and she needed to return to the States to help care for him, it became obvious that Evelyn needed to make a decision about returning to the States, as well. The authorities were increasingly unwilling to renew her visa, since she was an unaccompanied foreign married woman with dependent children. She made up her mind to go.

She knew it was the right decision, but there was so much to do. This was harder even than when she had gone to Pretoria. She would now be half a world away from her husband! But it had to be done. She took care of the many last details, gathered the kids and the suitcases, and resolutely set out. She was learning to trust the Lord in new ways.

The four of them traveled to North America in March 1976. Evelyn and the children stayed with family in the United States and Canada until my release. Lorraine had previously returned to the States to begin her home assignment.

Around that same time, there seemed to be a break in the logjam and people began to be released from the prison. We didn't see police agents coming for interviews, nor were inmates taken to the judiciary police offices to clarify statements, something we had anticipated. But people began to be released. Hope was renewed!

The first group of prisoners to be released were Portuguese nationals living in Mozambique. People of Portuguese origin were Portuguese citizens and may have lived in Mozambique for many generations. During this time many returned to Portugal.

On April 21, the three Brazilians in the prison, including Don Milam's colleague, Clécius, were called to the prison's police office. They were told that they would be released to go home if they could obtain plane tickets. It didn't take long for the three to find the resources, and we rejoiced with them as they were released.

Scattered among the prisoners were Africans from other countries who had come to Mozambique for one reason or another. Some came to participate in the socialist revolution and had been rounded up and imprisoned. Usually, these men were released quietly, and we didn't learn much of their stories.

Mozambicans who had been chosen by the FRELIMO party to prepare themselves to take positions in the new government had been sent to schools in East Germany and Russia for training. Their intent was to return and help rebuild the country after Independence. They, too, were rounded up and imprisoned. Many were frustrated that their local knowledge plus academic preparation in a socialist country was being wasted.

President Machel visited the prison after Don's and my release, and the plight of these bright students was brought up. He called them traitors who refused to take up arms against the Portuguese. Several comments were publicized nationally asserting that these traitors deserved death. They were among the most westernized of the black Africans, easy to get along with, and completely committed to Marxist-Leninism. During our discussions, they could be counted on to hold to the official Communist line, despite feeling betrayed.

In April, there was another flurry of activity which gave a sense of hope that something important was happening. It was during these days that two of our Nazarene colleagues, André Chilengue and Rev. Manuel Tshambe, were released.

On the afternoon of Tuesday, April 27, Don, and I, along with several others, were called to the commandant's office. The police agent first verified our names. He then asked if we wanted to go home. We didn't take time to ask what other options there were, but we did ask if Armand was also to be released. The agent replied that his name wasn't on the list.

After the meeting, as Don and I headed back to our cell we were thrilled to think that our prayers were being answered. But the reality soon sank in that when we left the prison, we would be leaving Armand behind. If there had been some way of his being allowed to go in our stead, we— either one—would have made the switch.

Within a short while, the US ambassador arrived to speak with the three of us. It was the first time since we'd been incarcerated that we would see and be introduced to any of the consulate or embassy staff. The ambassador told us he would get airline tickets for the three of us, with the hopes that at the last minute, the Mozambican authorities would allow Armand to join us.

He indicated that the tickets would be for the next available flight. That sounded good, but we knew that flights out of the country were booked months in advance and that it might be some time before we could leave. Sometimes people were notified on the Sunday evening radio news bulletin that they were being expelled from the country. But it would often take several days before their flights could be arranged.

With anticipation and hope, we got ready anyway. We spent the rest of the day preparing to leave and saying farewell to fellow prisoners. A number had heard our news and came by to congratulate us.

When Don and I remembered the promise of the prison authorities to return our books and Bibles when we left, we arranged to get them back. However, we left most of the reading materials with Armand, including copies of *National Geographic* someone had sent. Items that had been stored since our early days in the prison were dragged out from under the beds. We found clothes that Evelyn and Micki had brought us before they left the country.

****

Whenever Armand learned that a foreign prisoner was going to be released, he would contact him to see if he would be willing to mail a letter to his wife. Armand wrote these letters late into the night, catching Pauline up on news about himself and the others she knew who were in prison, and giving assurance of his health and his love for her. He would write using as many words as he could fit on a page. He would then wrap the letter in a piece of plastic and roll it as small as possible, with her address on the outside. Opening the crimped end of a toothpaste tube, he would remove some of the toothpaste, insert the note, and then refill it. Colgate South Africa used metallic tubes which made it easy to re-crimp them. Then the tube of toothpaste was delivered to the departing prisoner.

Armand prepared a note for Pauline to go with us that night just in case the ambassador's hopes for our speedy release were realized.

April 28 dawned with a lot of excitement. It intensified when the director sent word that we would be picked up to go to the airport at 9:00 am. Our flight to freedom was scheduled for 4:05 pm. We finished packing the old musty suitcases that had been stuffed under our beds and waited anxiously.

Evelyn was wrestling with her own hopes. She had begun to sense a prompting from the Lord that I would be released in April. A year earlier, the Mozambique mission council had approved April for us to go on home assignment. She was already home and this special month of celebrating her birthday and Easter would be a great time to welcome her husband. His release would be a special birthday present and a resurrection miracle. She continued to wait and to pray.

Jerald Johnson made several trips to southern Africa to advocate for our release. Usually, he would contact Evelyn. One time, Evelyn told Dr. Johnson that I was going to be released in April. She reported that he shook his head, saying it was a lot more complex a situation than anyone knew. Yet, I found myself on April 28, 1976, sitting on the edge of my bed in a prison in Mozambique awaiting a ride in a police car. I was going home to see my family!

At the airport, Don and I were met by Ambassador DuPree, given temporary travel documents and tickets, and boarded the plane. As we lifted off, it was hard to leave Armand behind, but I remember musing, "Mozambique, I hope I never see you again!"

About an hour later, the aircraft landed in Johannesburg at the Jan Smuts (now Oliver R. Thambo) International Airport. What a surprise to learn that many friends, including several of our missionary colleagues, were at the airport to greet us. It was great to see them again. Since we didn't have South African visas—they had long since expired—someone from the US embassy in Pretoria brought us travel documents and outgoing tickets, and we headed for our flight to Paris. After a refueling stop in Libreville in the Congo Republic, we had an early morning arrival at Charles de Gaulle Airport.

After a short layover and a little shopping, we were growing excited to be heading to New York and home. The eight-and-a-half-hour crossing of the Atlantic seemed to take forever. What a joy to finally see our wives after our long separation.

We turned our attention to Dr. Johnson, and other denominational and nearby district leaders. Then it was on to a crowd of well-wishers who were waiting for us. Photos were taken and songs sung. I went through the motions. I felt like I was finally home—and that was a good thing—but I felt numb, maybe in some kind of shock. It felt like a dream from which I might soon awaken. Could it be true that I was no longer behind those concrete walls? What had transpired in just a few hours was beyond comprehension.

Dr. Johnson and his staff had arranged for Evelyn and me to spend the night and next day in New York City. It was so special to have a few hours together before seeing the children and all that we were beginning to envision ahead of us. The superintendent of the Eastern Latin America district, José Cardona, and his wife, Adelaida, took us the next morning for a brief tour of New York City, and we enjoyed lunch in the World Trade Center.

God and the Church of the Nazarene hadn't forgotten us. Reports down through the years have confirmed that our names were often mentioned in prayer in Nazarene churches and homes all over the world. We even discovered that congregations of other denominations were faithfully praying. Those who were part of that great prayer effort still remind me about it. It continues to touch me deeply. The evil one told us that no one knew, and no one cared. How wrong, how very wrong! The One who promised to be with us was faithful to His promise.

11

Navigating Post-Prison Realities

One would think that being released from prison would be the end of the story. The prison experience, though in no way pleasant, in many ways was easier for my family and me than the period of time that followed. Suddenly, I found myself elevated to the status of celebrity. God had called me to be a missionary. I had not signed up for this!

The second day in the US, Evelyn and I caught a flight to Vancouver, British Columbia. This caused confusion as people thought we were Canadians. My parents, Raymond and Hazel Friberg, had been called from the State of Washington to pastor the Church of the Nazarene in Abbotsford, British Columbia. When Evelyn received word that I was being released, she left our two children with them and flew to New York City. Even Lorraine Schultz, our Mozambique missionary colleague, who was in British Columbia on her deputation tour, joined those who came to welcome us upon our arrival there. In subsequent days we heard from many of the area churches. There was a real outpouring of love.

It was in Abbotsford where I first began to feel the conflict between the solitude that I sought in order to recover from the prison ordeal, and the deeply-felt need to thank the church for her faithful support and advocacy on our behalf.

The US Ambassador warned me to be cautious about comments I made concerning the situation in Mozambique and our prison experience. Armand and various other Christian workers were still imprisoned. So, while I felt a strong desire to thank the church for her support, I knew I needed to guard carefully what I said. In those pre-Internet days, news didn't travel fast, but things said in the United States or Canada could easily reach the ears of government authorities in a country on the other side of the globe. Those words could both jeopardize Armand's safety and make negotiations for his release much more difficult. I was constantly on guard during the next five months until his release.

The need to get settled and find some sort of normalcy was soon evident. Evelyn, our young children Gayla about to turn 5, Mike 2½, and I needed time to get reacquainted. We all longed for some sense of order in our lives as well as find a place to make a home.

While the children were with my parents, one of the church families took them up into the mountains along the British Columbia-Washington border. There they saw snow for the first time. They felt genuinely loved by our Abbotsford friends and family.

A few days after we arrived in British Columbia, we packed up our few suitcases and headed south to Washington State in a borrowed car. I had graduated from high school in the Seattle area, and we were still members of the Sumner Church of the Nazarene where I had pastored before we left for Mozambique. We also had several friends in that area.

We decided to live in the Seattle suburb of Auburn, not far from Sumner. Being close to the Seattle-Tacoma International Airport was a big help for upcoming travel during my home assignment.

We found an apartment to rent in Auburn that met our needs, and we began the search for beds, tables, and the many other necessary items it takes to furnish a home. We had left a few personal items in the area when we left in 1971, so we gathered what we had stored and began to set up our home. Since we were settling in Auburn, we decided to transfer our membership to the Auburn Church of the Nazarene.

All of us had adjustments to make. On one occasion when our kids were with family members, they insisted they needed "serviettes" before they could eat. Their hosts asked if they meant a napkin. They insisted they did not. In Africa a napkin is a diaper; a serviette is a napkin. It created some healthy laughter.

In my post-prison days, it was very difficult to make decisions. Though there had been very few attempts at mind control and brainwashing, not having to make decisions for eight months had a negative effect. I had difficulty deciding on housing, travel, and a thousand other things.

****

Nazarene missionaries on home assignment create a "deputation" fund and are expected to visit churches and speak about their work. The fund would be used for vehicles, special projects, and additional expenses on the field upon returning. Encouraging continued support of the General Budget (now World Evangelism Fund), eliciting prayer support, as well as maintaining contact between the field and the global church, lay behind this expectation.

I had been selected by the Mozambique mission council to serve as their representative to the young people's convention at the Dallas quadrennial General Convention. It would be held in June, and we needed to make plans for getting to Texas.

On a trip to Nampa, Idaho, to visit Evelyn's sister Doris and her husband, we were invited to attend the last chapel of the school year at Northwest Nazarene College. We were greeted by students as well as faculty and staff, some of whom we knew from our time there as students a few years before. It was a very emotional experience. As years have passed, young people who were in that service have told us of the impact of seeing someone for whom they had prayed for such a long time, and to see God's answer.

While in Nampa, we were able to find a car which seemed to meet our needs, so we bought it. Our transportation to Dallas was set. We made arrangements with one of my brothers—Theron, and his wife, Scherlie—for Gayla and Michael to stay with them in California while we attended the conference.

Dr. Johnson asked if we would be willing to make an appearance at the Sunday afternoon mission service that opened the General Assembly. This didn't seem too daunting, so we agreed to delay our departure for Bakersfield to pick up the children.

A few days before the mission service, Dr. Johnson asked if we would be willing to do more than appear and actually speak a few words in the service. This significantly ramped up the anxiety level, since 35,000 people were expected to attend. We got through the experience all right, but we were now fully on the way to being celebrities. A reporter for a local newspaper wanted to interview us, and it quickly became clear how important it was to be cautious about words and attitudes. This level of public exposure was an altogether new experience for us.

People recognized us as we walked back and forth between our hotel and the convention center. One particularly memorable experience was when a delegation from Asia stopped us, and together we thanked the Lord for my release. A much fuller understanding of the church's investment in us through prayer and personal concern became very clear that day. A little of what it means to belong to a connectional denomination was verified.

As a result of being in Dallas, a number of speaking invitations came to me. The deputation schedule quickly filled up, and soon I found myself scheduled to crisscross

North America. After the enforced separation from my family while in prison, I was soon separated from them again for long periods. Evelyn was left without a partner in raising the children, and we all became very frustrated. I was experiencing the hospitality of generous North American Nazarenes. I was a guest in a number of beautiful homes and met many wonderful people, while my family was living in the simplicity of rather temporary housing and again separated from me.

When I would return home, I wanted to hide out and not interact with others. My family was ready to go out, shop, and do family things away from our small apartment. My brothers spoke to me about cancelling my speaking schedule, but my strong sense of responsibility kept driving me. I didn't want to let anyone down.

But the Lord knew our plight and through two events, my schedule changed. A general slowdown occurred when we discovered that Evelyn was pregnant and was due to have a child in April or May 1977.

Then, on a Sunday evening in February, I was the guest of a wonderful pastoral family in Kentucky when the phone rang. It was Evelyn, crying. My first thought was that she had lost the baby, but that wasn't the problem. She told me that our apartment had caught fire! She had taken the children for a Sunday evening activity at church, and someone contacted her to let her know. Friends rushed her and the children home in time to see the roof collapse. I immediately cancelled a district tour in Wisconsin and flew home to be with my family. The Auburn church pastor, Jerry Skidgel, his lovely wife, and their two daughters welcomed us into their home—which was a wonderfully safe and healing experience. The church people sifted through the rubble and took items home to clean, saving nearly everything personal. We were blessed to find another apartment nearby.

As Evelyn's due date got closer, I took a couple weeks of paternity leave to be with the family. But one district was rather insistent that I keep their scheduled tour because of their close involvement in our lives. I consented.

While I was on that tour, I got "the call." I asked our good friend, Betty Skidgel, to take Evelyn to the hospital while I rushed back to Washington, hoping to make it in time. But our little Lynnée arrived before I could get there. That I had missed the birth of both our daughters was especially difficult for Evelyn. Gayla was born in Washington while I was in Illinois at New Missionary Orientation, and now I was in Canada when Lynnée was born. Thankfully, I was with Evelyn and Gayla when Mike was born in Pretoria soon after our arrival in southern Africa.

In September 1976, while on a deputation tour in Southern California, I was excited to receive a phone call from the World Mission office. They wanted to notify me that Armand was about to be released and would soon be back in the United States. The call came during a meeting of local mission presidents from the Los Angeles District at Pasadena First Church. What joy erupted when the announcement of his release was made! They were so excited that they raised enough money for Evelyn and me to fly to New York to join Pauline in welcoming Armand home. In church after church, I had been urging people to continue praying for him, for the Lord's protection, and his release. Now, it was happening! In a few hours, we were going to be able to see him, hopefully well and safe. We could only say, "Thanks be to God!" Even though I still needed to be careful after that not to jeopardize the security of the Mozambican church, it felt wonderful that I would now be able to speak more fully of our imprisonment.

A second wave of rejoicing broke out when Armand and Pauline went on a tour of Nazarene congregations in the United States and Canada to celebrate our release. Armand's prison letters hidden in toothpaste tubes had reached Pauline and they were gathered into a book entitled, *The Toothpaste Express*. It was widely distributed on their tour.

****

I remember my frustrations upon my return to the United States, at not knowing exactly what I felt about everything. I didn't see any immediate application of what I had been through as it related to the life of the church. As time has passed, I have had a growing sense of purpose from it all. The Lord has given me things to say which have served to inspire and challenge the church. I am now enjoying a sense of usefulness for the Kingdom, though not in the usual evangelistic, discipleship, or mission mobilization sense.

With the many questions, I have had occasions to reflect on God's work. I was made aware of how our imprisonment had helped the Mozambican church. A few years after my release, field leaders from Mozambique met in Swaziland. I joined them from South Africa where we were serving. During our meeting, I learned that the Mozambican church had been encouraged by our willingness to stay with them even when things got difficult for us. The church felt we helped them through our imprisonment as we were no longer in authority over them but had learned to suffer with them. Even though we were now serving in another country, this encouragement and acknowledgement of their love and perseverance was wonderful. What a joy to learn that the Mozambicans still considered us their missionaries. Through the years, the Lord enabled His Mozambican church to work effectively. A strong church had been established under national leaders so when we missionaries had to leave, they were able to carry on the work of the church on their own.

Dr. Johnson and the World Mission staff began to look with us at the options for our future missionary service. We felt a strong sense of calling to return to Africa. During this time, Pastor Earl Lee invited us to serve on staff at Pasadena First Church of the Nazarene. As much as we would have enjoyed working with the Lees, who were dear friends, we didn't feel free to accept their invitation. They would soon experience their own prison journey when their son Gary was imprisoned in Tehran, Iran, through much of 1980 as a member of the US Embassy staff.

Because we had a working knowledge of the Portuguese language, we were asked if we would consider going to Portuguese-speaking Cabo Verde or Brazil. But, in spite of my initial reaction of not wanting to ever go back to Mozambique, we felt strongly that our future was in southern Africa. Eventually, recognizing my interest and aptitude in office work as well as literature, we made a renewed commitment to ministry in Africa, and we moved in 1978. My role would be to serve as the editorial coordinator overseeing the literature work for all of Africa while living in Johannesburg.

Due to the expense of production and marketing as well as the complexity of languages used by Nazarenes across the continent, the decision had been made before our arrival to close the Shirley Press, thus ending book printing. The focus would be on curriculum and literature development. The Africa Editorial Board was formed with men and women representing the church and the mission, and I was brought in as the young and inexperienced editorial coordinator. Changes came along the way when Dr. Richard Zanner opened the regional office where I would work, and the Editorial Board became Africa Nazarene Publications.

The assignment put us back on the continent, where we had felt so much connection with people and places. We were able to raise our children in the complexity of a multi-cultural world, with missionary and national friends from across the whole cultural spectrum. Evelyn and I and the children enjoyed our eight years in Johannesburg, South

Africa, while I worked in literature and then as faculty at Africa Nazarene Theological College.

The educational ministry of the church was a good fit for me, and I felt I was where I needed to be. Following our years in Johannesburg, we were transferred to the theological school in Swaziland. It was a shock to our systems to move from Maputo and Johannesburg with their millions of inhabitants to the small community of Siteki. Both Evelyn and I found places of ministry with the faculty and students, as well as other groups of people living in the Kingdom of Swaziland (now Eswatini). Evelyn became deeply connected to a group of refugees who had made their way to the peaceful kingdom from their troubled countries of origin. The Swazi government placed them in camps that had been built for refugees from Mozambique who had fled the violence in the civil war. I became involved with groups gathered in sugar plantation communities.

It was during this time that our children completed their secondary education and headed off to Northwest Nazarene College (now University) for their bachelor studies.

****

Following our release from prison, Mozambique slid into a long and destructive civil war when other political parties began to struggle with FRELIMO for control. At the end of an eighteen-year period, the two major contenders, RENAMO (Mozambique National Resistance) and FRELIMO, came together to form a government of national unity. Suspicions and differences of opinion continued for several years, especially after the crash of the plane on the Mozambique-South African border that killed Mozambique's president, Samora Machel.

Not only did peace come eventually, but the direction of the country changed to a multi-party government with a free-market economy. It meant that congregations were freed to meet openly, and some properties were restored for the church to use. The Bible college was now reopened, renamed *Seminário Nazareno de Moçambique* (SNM) and moved from "up-country" Tavane to Maputo. Frank Howie, now serving as the mission director, felt free to return to Mozambique to encourage the church. At first, it was still dangerous to travel the roads between countries. In fact, on one occasion, someone shot at Frank's car but it still "limped" into Maputo for meetings.

At last, three missionary couples were able to enter the country and live and work: field director Frank (and Heather) Howie; Doug and Elaine Perkins (son of Floyd and Libby);

and educators David and Rhoda Restrick. A volunteer couple, Johnny and Carol Fillmore, who were living in Maputo, coordinated short-term missions and building projects. Then, the work in northern and central Mozambique began to develop quickly. Jonas and Lousada Mulate from southern Mozambique moved to northern Mozambique to work among the Makhuwa people. They were at the time one of the largest unreached people groups in the world.

Missionaries Jim and Arla Jeanne Buchanan settled in the city of Tete in northern Mozambique, Carlos and Sylvia Bauza of Argentina in Quelimane, and David and Marquita Mosher in the city of Nampula, where they worked with the Mulates. They were all involved in district and leadership development.

****

At times I have thought of the effect our imprisonment has had on various groups. Did I have something more to say to the church? What did God yet want to do through me? After such intensive focus on telling the story in many different settings and congregations from Vermont to Southern California and Alaska to Florida, I put the story aside for several years. For several furloughs, my focus was to talk of the mission of the Church and our part as Nazarene believers in it.

But finally, near the end of my ministry under appointment by the World Mission Department, a friend who had invested heavily in Mozambique ministry, Randy Craker, told me he thought it was time for me to start telling the story again. It seemed a divine confirmation of a desire that had been growing in me. I felt free once again to encourage the saints with the message: God knows how to make and keep His promises. The "I will be with you" promise in Matthew's version of the Great Commission command of Jesus is just as true today as it was in those days. The prisons in which people find themselves are not all made of cement and steel.

Not long before Independence, at a district meeting at the Maputo Central Church, one of the district leaders took the opportunity to express the attitude of the African church in times of difficulty. He had fastened oranges to a branch, and in his illustration, vigorously waved the branch back and forth. Some of the oranges fell off the branch, but most remained firmly attached. He said that the winds of adversity will come, and some will fall away, but most will hold on in faithfulness to the Lord and His Church.

In early 2009, as we were preparing to leave Africa for our final home assignment and retirement from missionary service, our former student and field strategy coordinator for Mozambique, Paulo Moises Sueia, invited us to attend the Maputo District Assembly. He presented us a beautiful reproduction, in native Mozambican wood, of a Distinguished Service Award, along with many kind words for our years of service in Mozambique.

It serves as a reminder of the joy of serving and the gratitude we have to the Lord, the church, and the people for all they have done.

Epilogue

The year 2022 marked the one-hundredth anniversary of the arrival of the first Nazarene missionaries in Mozambique and the founding of what has become the largest national Church of the Nazarene in Africa Region.

As a result of the faithfulness of national Mozambicans and their missionary colleagues, the church has grown from small beginnings in the southern part of the country to cover the entire nation. Today there are nearly 2000 churches in 34 districts, with a total of 228,000 members. These are the churches that organized and gathered separately then nationally to celebrate the *Centenário* October 28-29, 2022, in Tavane, the site of the first mission station and district center. Leaders of the church in the country and across the continent, as well as former missionaries and others were invited to join with the Mozambicans as they celebrated. Representatives from the national and local government as well as other religious groups also joined in.

Not only was the event a gathering of the national church, with times of worship, a musical extravaganza, and delicious meals, but it was also a time of recollection and rehearsal of the challenges the church has confronted and the blessings it has experienced through the years. Several national historians prepared discussions for these events. Then, since the first-generation pioneers had all passed on to glory, second-generation leaders reminded those in attendance of God's blessings and the direction forward with the challenging theme, "The Best is Yet to Come!"

I was blessed to see Admirado and Celeste Chaguala and their team planning, organizing, and facilitating a very complex event. Danny Gomis the Regional Director, Aderito Fereira the Field Strategy Coordinator, and two African-born General Superintendents, Eugenio Duarte and Filimao Chambo, were in attendance. A large tent was set up for the services, meals prepared, water provided, and sleeping tents set up as over 3,000 Nazarenes came from across Mozambique to celebrate a century of God's faithfulness and blessing upon the Church of the Nazarene. In the middle of the mission station, the Glenn Grose Memorial Church of the Nazarene building stands as a solid reminder of the foundational years. And now under the tent, the amplified sound, the modern music, the big screens, and fancy lighting equipment brought us back to the present.

Many of those in attendance whom I knew personally had been my students at the Nazarene College of Theology in Siteki, Swaziland. They had gone to Swaziland to take advantage of that college's ability to provide English-medium instruction on the bachelor's level and now were serving as leaders in the church and the pastoral training school. This included not only pastors and district superintendents, but also a former field strategy coordinator. What a joy to see Samuel Chone, Gilberto Langa, Margarida Langa, Arsénio Mandlate, Isaac Mandlate, Julião Matsinhe, Paulo Moises Sueia, and Adolfo Tembe, all of whom had been our students!

One of the biggest surprises for me was seeing the improvements in infrastructure so visible around the country: many new skyscrapers in Maputo and its suburbs, shopping malls and new housing development, a freeway that circled the city, bridges, and the port of Maputo busy with loading South African coal for shipment around the world.

Inside the cities the changes were not so dramatic since there had been development when we lived there. But now the two-track National Highway has become a paved road—at times a four-lane divided highway—heading north in the direction of the mission at Tavane. Only the last few kilometers remain unpaved, but they are better maintained than in years past. The Church of the Nazarene mirrors the same forward-looking enthusiasm and development.

Among the people I was thankful to see at the celebration was André Chilengue. At the time of this prison story, he was a young high school student working for the Dolls. Now he was the district superintendent of one of the southern Mozambique districts. When I had seen him in 2009, he was warm and welcoming, rejoicing in the Lord's provision in his life even when his wife died. He gave me such a welcome hug. I noticed he didn't look particularly well, but the moment passed quickly as we greeted each other and visited. Imagine my surprise a few weeks after returning home from the celebration to hear that his health had suddenly worsened, and he had passed away due to complications of diabetes. What a shock to learn that this tie to my history and the history of the Church of the Nazarene in Mozambique was not to be seen on earth again. This was a strong reminder that only what's done for the Lord will last.

Returning to Mozambique was life changing in many ways. I was reminded again that in all things God works for good, even when it seems like things are falling apart. The Mozambique church is flourishing, and this celebration helped me to see that our small role contributed to the success.

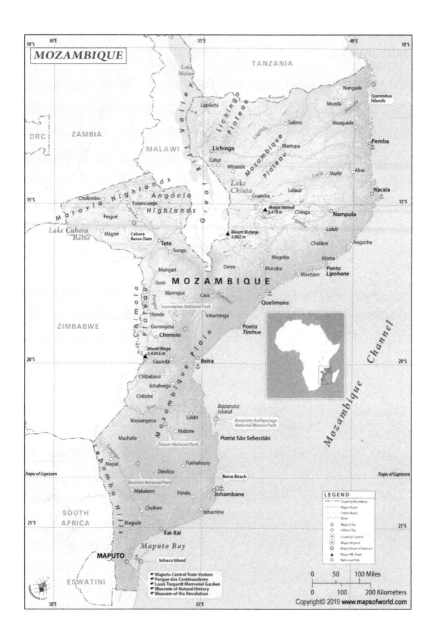

MOZAMBIQUE